From Reviews

★ ★ ★ ★

'An Interesting Travel Memoir'

"A Maverick Himalayan Way by adventurer and author Mary Jane Walker is a very interesting travel memoir. The Himalayas and the Indian Subcontinent has a rich culture, unique tradition, glorious past, heritage monuments, magnificent forts & palaces, beautiful temples, rippling sand dunes, wildlife sanctuaries & national parks, traditional villages, palace hotels, heritage hotels, excellent hospitality and of course generous people. Traveling in different cities and tourist destinations of this royal and imperial land would be a unique lifetime experience."

'Piaras' Amazon Vine Voice Reviewer, 24 May 2019

★ ★ ★ ★

'A maverick Himalayan way, way too short'

". . . I now answer the question most prospective readers would like to read: is this book worth reading?

"My answer is yes. If I found this book a good read even with my intimate knowledge of two of the three countries covered, people not familiar with these countries should find it even more engrossing."

Venky Iyer, conclusion of Amazon review, 4 August 2019

A NOMAD IN NEPAL

And the Lands Next Door

Mary Jane Walker

Author's Dedication

I would like to dedicate this book to all the cultures of the Himalayan region — you are many. Thank you for inviting me into your homes. It has been a journey I hope to continue.

Mary Jane Walker is a writer of historically well-informed travel narratives that come with an autobiographical flavour.

Like all Kiwis, Mary Jane was raised on tales of Sir Edmund Hillary's climbing of Mount Everest alongside the Sherpa Tenzing Norgay, and of Hillary's subsequent good works among the impoverished Sherpa community in Nepal.

But she never felt the urge to go to the Himalayas herself, until friends persuaded her to go with them on a cheap trek up to Everest Base Camp, in Nepal.

What the heck, she thought—let's go! But if she was going to go to the Himalayas, she wasn't going to confine herself to the Everest region, or even to Nepal.

In *A Nomad in Nepal and the Lands Next Door*, Mary Jane *updates A Maverick Himalayan Way*, the earlier edition of this book. She describes her adventures in several parts of upland and Himalayan Nepal: the Everest region, Manaslu, Annapurna, and the Kathmandu Valley. In the Chitral district of Pakistan, bordering Afghanistan, where the Hindu Kush mountains continue the Himalayas westward. In Sikkim, a once-independent principality east of Nepal. And finally, once more in Nepal, in the low-altitude, subtropical, Chitwan region.

Email: maryjanewalker@a-maverick.com
Facebook: facebook.com/amavericktraveller
Instagram: @a_maverick_traveller

Linkedin: Mary Jane Walker
Pinterest: amavericktraveller
Twitter: @Mavericktravel0

Author's website: **a-maverick.com**

Published 2021 by:

Mary Jane Walker
A Maverick Traveller Ltd
PO Box 44 146, Point Chevalier, Auckland 1246, New Zealand
www.a-maverick.com
Email: maryjanewalker@a-maverick.com

ISBN: 978-0-473-58219-7 (mobi), 978-0-473-58217-3
(softcover POD), 978-0-473-58218-0 (epub), 978-0-473-58220-3 (digital audiobook)

Disclaimer
This book is a travel memoir, not an outdoors guide. Although the author and publisher have made every effort to ensure that the information in this book was correct at the time of publication, the author and publisher do not assume and hereby disclaim any liability to any party for any loss, damage, or

disruption caused by errors or omissions, whether such errors or omissions result from negligence, accident, or any other cause. Some names have also been changed to disguise and protect certain individuals.

Notes on Images

All maps have north at the top and have been drawn for this book by Chris Harris unless otherwise credited. All photographs in the book are the property of Mary Jane Walker unless otherwise credited.

Covers and Fonts

The front cover includes a NASA public domain satellite image of Nepal on 27 October 2002 from Visible Earth imagery via Wikimedia Commons, the author credited as Jacques Descloitres, MODIS Rapid Response Team, NASA/GSFC. The fonts used for the title on the front cover and spine are Impact and Impact Condensed. The interior text of this print edition is typeset throughout in Garamond.

Author's tip: How to see images from this book in colour and at higher resolution

Each chapter of this book links to blog posts on my website, which contain the images in the chapter and additional images and videos in some cases as well, in colour and at higher resolution.

There's plenty more on my website, too!

a-maverick.com

MARY JANE WALKER

Contents

Nepal and surrounding lands in the Indian subcontinent

Introduction

TEN years ago, I really knew nothing about Nepal, its neighbouring lands, and the great Himalayan mountain range they share.

I knew that Sir Edmund Hillary and the ever-smiling Sherpa, Tenzing Norgay, had been the first to conquer the mountain we call Everest. And that was about the sum of my knowledge.

Most of what I know now is what I have learnt from going to these lands in the years since.

When I was in a hiking club, sometime around 2010, I sat through a presentation on the Himalayas. I sat in front of a screen where photo after photo of great peaks such as Everest, Annapurna and Ama Dablam were projected. And the people I saw in these photos were different from Tenzing.

Nobody was smiling. People were suffering from either altitude sickness or frostbite, and they looked miserable. There was talk of yak poo on the trails, and of staying in tents. Goodness, I thought. Why would anyone even bother to go there? It did not sound appealing.

Hiking presentations did nothing to make me want to go to Nepal. I had spent a good part of my life trekking in New Zealand, and I didn't see the point in going to Nepal. That is, until a couple of friends invited me to join them on a group tour. The tour sounded ridiculously cheap, only $1,500 for seventeen days plus $1,150 for the return flight (American dollars, that is; though New Zealand has its own currency, all references to dollars in this book are to US dollar prices). I hadn't been out of New Zealand in a while. Suspecting that I have a wanderlust gene in me, I thought I might as well spend six months away. So, I asked, why should I confine myself to Nepal?

The tallest Himalayan peaks lie in Nepal. But the mighty mountain range traverses five countries in a sort of belt with mountain forests just south of the higher peaks, and the more arid lands of China's Tibetan autonomous region (Tibet) and Xinjiang province to the north.

The ecology of the Himalayan belt is rich and diverse. On the front cover of this book, you can see a section of the belt consisting mainly of parts of Nepal along with Tibet to the north and the Indian plains to the south. But the distinctive Himalayan belt runs all the way from Pakistan in the west, where it becomes the Hindu Kush range, to Bhutan in the east.

On the facing page there is a wider satellite view from the same source as the image on the cover. The view extends as far as the confluence of the Ganges, known in Bangladesh as the Padma, with the Brahmaputra River at bottom right. Both of these important rivers have their sources in the Himalayas, as does the Indus, the most important river in Pakistan.

'The Himalayas', NASA public domain image via Visible Earth, with north (Tibet) at top approximately. Nepal is in the middle, and Bhutan at right. The Himalayan belt shown also continues westward into the Indian state of Uttarakhand, and, to the left of the picture, into the Indian state of Himachal Pradesh, the divided lands of Jammu and Kashmir, and northern Pakistan including Chitral. NASA image reference details Nepal.A2002300.0505, taken 27 October 2002, credit to Jacques Descloitres, MODIS Rapid Response Team, NASA/GSFC.

I decided that if I were to go to that part of the world, I would go to as many parts of it as I could. So, I went to Sikkim, which used to be a separate country until India annexed it in 1975. I went to Chitral in Pakistan, to Kashmir and to Dharamshala, in the Indian state of Himachal Pradesh. And I've gone three times to Nepal, so far. (Tibet and Bhutan are still on my to-do list.)

I saw and learnt a lot in Chitral. The Hindu Kush mountain range is majestic, and the scenery is breathtaking. The people are lovely – they're hospitable and peaceful. It's just a shame to see what the war in neighbouring Afghanistan has brought about.

I certainly enjoyed Kashmir, a territory divided between Pakistan, India and China. I was enchanted by Sufi Islam and how its followers practised their religion by celebrating music. It was quite different from the more austere kinds where women can't dance, and music isn't celebrated.

And it was a special experience to visit Dharamshala, in the nearby Indian state of Himachal Pradesh, where the Dalai Lama is based.

Nepal was wonderful, so much so that I visited more than once. I love the Tibetan Buddhism which the Sherpas practise, and their view of life. I love the smiling children – the children smiled a lot! But not so much the smiling Sherpas, because life there isn't much about smiles right now. The movie *Sherpa* highlights the hardships they face, brought about in part by the death of many males in that community. These days, the people of Nepal, including the Sherpas, are being devastated by Covid-19. If the more prosperous countries insist on fully patent-protecting their vaccines and don't roll them out cheaply to the rest of the world, the politicians of these countries will have blood on their hands and will be setting their own populations up for further outbreaks and the evolution of new strains, as well.

I have had my share of disappointments in Nepal, and I have had uplifting moments. I have been to the bases of some of the world's highest peaks and seen some of the most majestic landscapes on the planet.

I absolutely loved Sikkim. It was a magical place. I celebrated Gautama Buddha's birthday there and attended a funeral, getting a taste of everyday life. I saw beautiful sights and met wonderful people.

Statue of Tenzing Norgay at the Himalayan Mountaineering Institute, Darjeeling, India. Photo by Colin Ashe (2006, cropped by PPlecke), via Wikimedia Commons, CC-BY-SA 2.5

Buddhist Prayers creating a 'Mani Wall', near Mount Everest. These have to be passed on the left side, in order to respect a sacred principle of clockwise movement as viewed from above.

Buddhist prayer wheels at Rumtek Monastery, Sikkim. These are rotated clockwise as well, as viewed from above. I saw similar ones at Tengboche, and smaller prayer wheels were very common. Photo by Sivakumar (2012), CC-BY-SA 3.0, Wikimedia Commons.

Wayside Shrine (top) and Mountaineers' Memorial (below), both in the Khumbu region, near Mount Everest

In all these places, I felt safe most of the time, though I am the kind of woman who can feel unsafe in the centre of

Auckland or Queenstown at night when it is not well lit. I think it is about how someone approaches these things; it's about how people travel and where they travel. I have always lived my life the way I wanted to and so I have done my fair share of travelling. The Himalayan region forms a strong part of my travel experience, and I would suggest that people go there.

Having said that, in the second-to-last chapter I describe some unpleasant guiding experiences based on real first-hand knowledge. The quality of trail guides in Nepal is quite variable, and although the guides and porters have very legitimate grievances (which I go into in Chapter Six), at the same time, the trekker can be taken for a ride, or even propositioned, as I was.

Someday, I would like to trek on the Great Himalaya Trails – to travel this formidable mountain range from one end to another. You can't get enough of the Himalayas!

The Great Himalaya Trails (branded as such) run most of the length of Nepal: from Kanchenjunga, the world's third highest mountain, on the border of Nepal and Sikkim, westward to western Nepal. There is a high trade route and a low (cultural) route, though the word 'low' is relative here.

Life is in the mountains. They say that people force themselves to live in the moment by climbing mountains. Do we want to touch God? I have no idea.

Yet not all of Nepal is in the mountains! The capital, Kathmandu, is 1,400 metres above sea level (4,600 feet), but I travelled down from there to the Chitwan National Park on the border with India. Chitwan is an area of meandering rivers that is only about 200 metres or 600-odd feet above sea level. The national park is a famous wildlife preserve, literal tiger country. I talk about Chitwan in my final chapter, 'Batons for the Beasts', after the batons we were given in case we needed to fend off wild beasts!

I highly recommend the great many videos that are now on YouTube, and elsewhere, as the next best thing to being there wherever 'there' might be, and as essential preparation, these days, for going there!

Finally, make sure that you get all the relevant travel advisories, vaccinations, and insurance!

Web versions of content (blog posts with images and videos), and chapter notes

Here is a website version of this Introduction:

a-maverick.com/blog/introduction-to-a-nomad-in-nepal

Each successive chapter also links to one or more blog posts on my website in a similar fashion. These often contain more photographs than the same chapter in the book, in colour. And the blog posts also contain embedded videos in some cases.

If there are any notes intended to clarify chapter content, these will follow the website link for each chapter.

CHAPTER ONE

Himalayan History
Where East met West, and India collides with the North

THIS book is about my journey across landscapes renowned not only for their beauty but also for their cultures and religions. I went to Nepal because I was encouraged by friends to go on a group trek, and I found myself in love with learning. That is, with learning about the interrelations between nature and the peoples who had come to depend on their local environments, whether historically or in modern times.

The discoveries of diversity within the natural environment, cultural heritage and religions that I made during my trip around the Himalayan Region were surprising and inspiring.

I learnt that growing and cultivating rice is one of the oldest forms of farming in the world. I visited Buddhist and Hindu temples — the latter the temples of the oldest major religion in the modern world, a religion that dates back even to the time of the Indus Valley Civilisation in the Bronze Age.

I saw old traditions practised alongside modern ones. I visited Buddhist temples and monuments and saw how each culture brings a different element to bear. To me, it was more than just seeing these beautiful mountains up close or even walking through them, which is no easy feat. It was also about the people that live in their shadows, the cultures and ethnic groups that wake up and see them every day.

The discovery of trails, temples, jaw-dropping scenery and new cultures all went hand in hand when I visited the Himalayan mountains and surrounding areas.

I'd like to give a brief history, here, of the Himalayan region, and some of the relationships between the countries that are joined together by the mountains.

Asia is by far the biggest continent in the world. Migrations out of Asia led to the settlement of various areas, including the Pacific Islands, Hawaii and even New Zealand. Inter-continent migrations led to the rise and fall of empires, kingdoms, cultures and languages.

The Himalayan mountain ranges are among the most majestic I have ever seen. There are more than 110 peaks above 7,200 metres in elevation in the Himalayas, including the world's giant, Mt Everest. The Himalayas run for over 2,400 kilometres from Pakistan, where they merge into the Hindu Kush, through the disputed territory of Kashmir and the northernmost states of India, through Tibet (China), Nepal, Sikkim (India) and Bhutan, to the vicinity of Darjeeling in India's far north-east.

The countries that the Himalayas traverse vary in their cultural practices and religions, but I also saw similarities between them all.

When I went to Nepal, my aim was to do the base-camp trek on Mt Everest. It was almost like stepping back in time. Some of the people I saw on my trek still lived in nomad-like conditions in freezing temperatures in the foothills of the mountain. I was amazed at the lack of technology – they simply didn't need it with the reliance on animals as transport and the adherence to traditional ways of life. It was not as if I was surprised, but to see things first-hand gives you a whole new view on it all.

It got me interested in travelling through more of Asia and seeing as much as I could, getting my own insights on the people who live throughout.

Nepal – The Buddha's mostly Hindu birthplace

Nepalese culture is a beautiful example of tolerance. The Kathmandu Valley area was a concentration of a mixture of religious monuments from the Buddhist, Hindu, and Jain religions – a group of religions that have existed side by side for hundreds of years. The wider culture of the area dates back thousands of years.

Over 80% of Nepalese follow the Hindu faith, 9% are Buddhist, four and a half per cent are Muslim and 3% are Kirat Mundhum, a minority religion which worships Mother Nature.

There are over 29 million people in Nepal, nearly all of whom are ethnically related to Indian populations on the other side of Nepal's southern border and speak a similar language.

Even though most foreigners probably think of the Sherpas as the most distinctively 'Nepalese' people, amazingly enough, less than a quarter of a million of Nepal's citizens are Sherpas; a small and hitherto almost invisible minority of mountain-dwellers, which was thrust into the world spotlight by the rise of Himalayan climbing in the twentieth century.

The Sherpas aren't related to the inhabitants of India, being relatives of the Tibetans instead.

There are many major Hindu and Buddhist temples and other sacred structures within the Kathmandu Valley alone, some of them damaged or destroyed in Nepal's devastating 2015 earthquake, but many still standing. The sacred Bagmati River also runs through the Kathmandu Valley, bringing another element of historical and cultural value to the area.

Nepal, also known as the Kingdom of Gorkha, was the only Hindu kingdom in the world, and existed for over 240 years as a monarchy. In 2001, the royal family was murdered in a massacre carried out by the heir to the throne. He killed nine members of his family and then himself. The monarchy was abolished in 2008.

Nepal has always struggled for independence, from China and India, and even from Britain after Nepal lost the Anglo-Nepalese War in the nineteenth century. When the monarchy was abolished in 2008, so too was the official status of the Hindu religion. Nepal is now a secular state, although Hinduism remains the main religion.

Religion across is Asia is something I did not know much about. I thought I knew a lot until I got there and began to see it all for myself and to take in the details.

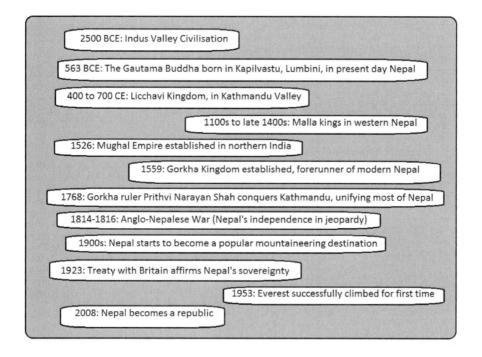

Timeline of Nepalese history (some dates approximate)

Without the Himalayas, Pakistan, Bangladesh, Nepal and northern India would all be a desert region with a comparatively small population, like Arabia, the Sahara, or the south-western USA and northern Mexico.

Being a desert is the norm in these latitudes. It is only the melting of huge amounts of ice and snow in the Himalayas and neighbouring mountain chains that keeps the rivers of northern India, Nepal, Bangladesh, and most of Pakistan flowing during the hottest and driest times of the year, just before the monsoon. And the monsoon is, itself, largely a by-product of the existence of the Himalayas.

A particularly well-watered area in lowland Nepal, which borders India and forms a national park within the foothills of the Himalayas – the Chitwan National Park – is one of the last wild areas where Bengal tigers can be found. This area shows the dependence of the wildlife, too, on the environments created and manipulated by the Himalayas. The rivers that are fed by the snow on the mountains flow through this area bringing water and therefore life and sustainability. The Chitwan National Park is one of the many national parks that depend on the Himalayas for survival and nourishment. I describe a visit to Chitwan in the last chapter of this book. An abundance of rivers nourishes wildlife in the Chitwan area, wildlife is protected from poachers by roughly a thousand soldiers of the Nepalese Army. The animals protected in Chitwan include the rare Indian Rhinoceros, whose skin folds in a way that makes it look like the animal is covered in separate plates of armour, as opposed to the more normal-looking hide of the various African rhino species.

People who've only seen African rhinos in wildlife documentaries sometimes think that the plates of armour in the Nuremberg artist Albrecht Dürer's famous 1515 depiction of a rhinoceros are a totally fanciful, made-up detail.

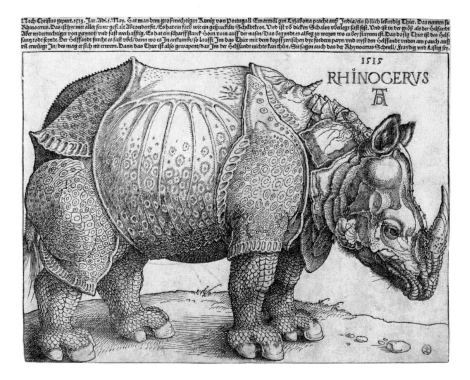

The Rhinoceros, by Albrecht Dürer. National Gallery of Art (USA) image, digitally enhanced, via Wikimedia Commons (public domain)

Well, actually, the rhinos of Chitwan *do* rather look like Dürer's fabulous beast. Dürer was sketching an Indian rhino that had lately turned up in Lisbon, a gift of the Sultan of Gujarat to the King of Portugal, and based his sketch on the descriptions by people who'd just seen it. In the circumstances, he did a pretty good job.

The point is that the Indian rhinoceros is so rare and exotic, that even today most people don't even know there is such a thing.

When I visited Nepal, I found that the people harboured no bad feelings towards other cultures, not even the British who were once so dominant in the region. The varieties of religions are interwoven into everyday society, and it was a brilliant place to meet Buddhist and Hindu people.

Islam and Christianity are minority religions here. The very first Christian missionary to Nepal was recorded in 1628. Missionaries were not allowed into Nepal during Prithvi Narayan Shah's rule in the 1700s, and so Hinduism flourished. Christians now make up just 1.4% of the population in Nepal.

Before I got there, I had imagined that Buddhism would be the major religion of Nepal. The founder of Buddhism, Siddhārtha Gautama, who lived and preached in and around the fifth century BCE, was the son of a chief of the Shakya clan, which was at the time based in and around the ancient (and modern) city of Lumbini in Nepal, just west of today's Chitwan National Park and just north of the present-day Indian border.

Where the Buddha was born (Lumbini) and died (Kushinagar) in relation to Kathmandu, Chitwan, and the modern international frontier

Siddhārtha Gautama – the Buddha or Lord Buddha – is reliably attested to have been born at Lumbini, which is now called Lumbini Sanskritik Municipality to give it its full name, Lumbini the cultural city. The Buddha is attested with equal reliability to have died at an advanced age (eighty, by one account) in Kushinagar, a town on the Ganges plain in India. Kushinagar is only a hundred kilometres from Lumbini, though the Buddha travelled much further afield during his most active days.

Buddhism has at least 500 million adherents in the world today, possibly more than a billion, though a precise number is impossible to come by. This is partly because of past discouragement of overt religious practice in China and other Communist countries in Asia, when sites of worship were not being more violently closed down. And partly also, because Buddhist worship is often fairly informal and may be combined with other faiths. So, it is likely that the lowest estimates of the number of Buddhists in the world are under-estimates, though nobody knows by how much.

The monks in their saffron robes and the smiling faces of the Buddha statues were a welcome sight in many of the countries I visited. I learnt that India and Nepal share a few similarities in their culture besides their main religions, like how they dress and that at some point they were both invaded by the Mughals, Muslim rulers of central Asian origin and with a strong Persian cultural influence, who built the Taj Mahal. Both countries were also under British control after the reign of the Mughals. India seems to have a longer recorded history than Nepal, but that is because Nepal was considered part of northern India many years ago. This relationship is the subject of the following section.

Nepal's ties with India

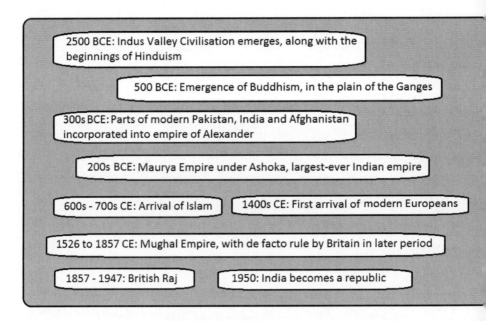

Timeline of the history of India (some dates approximate)

Since ancient times, the history of Nepal has been intimately bound up with that of India: the site of. one of the world's first major civilisations, the Indus Valley Civilisation, which peaked from 3,300 to 1,300 BCE. The Indus Valley Civilisation was a fascinating culture that was advanced in the sciences and arts, and which merged with other groups to create the Indian culture as it is today. The Indus Valley Civilisation covered an area that was not in only modern-day India, but also neighbouring Pakistan and Afghanistan.

India also saw more of Islam than Nepal. Muslim cultures from central Asia invaded frequently, bringing their religion with them.

The Himalayas created a barrier for India from invasions from the north (although this didn't stop the Mongolians in the 12th century). The ranges run through ten states of northern India, including Sikkim and Uttar Pradesh – some of the places I went to.

Hindu beliefs are thought to have begun during the time of the Indus Valley Civilisation. The Hindu religion is also historically bound up with the caste system in the Hindu-majority nations of India and Nepal. While modern governments have tried to abolish the deeply founded idea of caste, in India in particular, I found it still very prevalent among the Hindu populations of India. Ironically, in Nepal, I had more to do with Buddhist Sherpa minorities, as most Western trekkers would, and thus did not see so much of the Hindu side of Nepal.

Christianity constitutes the third-largest Indian religion, followed by 2.3 per cent of the population or in other words almost one per cent more than in Nepal.

India was one of the first countries in Asia to receive Christian missionaries. It is said that the faith was brought to India as early as 52 CE by Thomas the Apostle. By the sixth century it was an established religion, and quite strong to this day in the southern part of India. The Dalits ('broken people'), also historically known as Untouchables, at the bottom of the caste system in India and Nepal, also swell the ranks of Christian converts.

Roughly the same percentage of Nepal's population falls into the Dalit category as in India: about a sixth or a seventh.

Incidentally, the preferred legal and bureaucratic term for Dalits / Untouchables in Nepal and India is 'scheduled Castes'.

Islam, the second-largest religion in India, arrived through Arab traders in the seventh century. There is evidence that that Indians and Arabs had extensive trade relations, possibly even before the founding of Islam. The Muslim influence was then reinforced by way of central Asian invaders.

Buddhism is another of the religions that shaped the Indian culture early on in history. Buddhism flourished in India during the fourth century and made its way further afield to China, Japan, Korea, and Southern Asia, by traders along the famed Silk Road.

Some of the earliest Buddhist schools can be found in India, spreading there from what is now Nepal into the northern and southern states. Buddhism spread particularly rapidly through the central areas of Asia, including Afghanistan, under the Kushan Empire of the first centuries CE. Wanderers spread the religion further to Southeast Asia, as far as Vietnam, Cambodia, and the Philippines.

A Chinese Buddhist monk was one of the first recorded to make a religious pilgrimage to India. His name was Faxian and he travelled through India, Pakistan, Afghanistan, Sri Lanka and Nepal visiting sacred Buddhist sites. The popularity of

Buddhism and its transmission via the Silk Road began to decline as Hinduism became re-established as the core religion of India around the 700s CE.

This is a curious fact: that Buddhism arose in India and Nepal but enjoyed greatest success in East Asia. But anyhow, this explains what the colossal 'Bamyan Buddhas' that the Taliban so notoriously blew up some years ago were doing in Afghanistan, such a long way from the main centres of Buddhism today.

Sikkim was an interesting part of India. It became the 22nd state of India in 1975 so its merger with the larger country is fairly recent; it was independent before that. Sikkim sits high up in the Himalayas and shares a border with Nepal, with which it also shares a history of wars and invasions.

Along with nearby Bhutan, Sikkim remains an important Buddhist area. In the eighth century CE the patron Buddhist saint of Sikkim, Padmasambhava (one of the most famous historical figures in Tibetan Buddhism, also known as Guru Rinpoche), visited the area and prophesied a great Sikkim monarchy, which eventuated in the form of the Buddhist Chogyal rulers, who reigned over Sikkim from 1642 CE to 1975 CE. But in any case, the Rumtek Monastery remains of high importance and is one of the most sacred sites within Sikkim.

Close to Sikkim is the famous Indian hill city of Darjeeling. Until the beginning of the 1950s, Darjeeling, not Nepal, was the centre of Sherpa mountaineering. Tenzing Norgay, who conquered the mountain known to Westerners as Everest alongside Edmund Hillary in 1953, came from Darjeeling.

23

In the first half of the twentieth century Nepal was what was known as a 'hermit kingdom', suspicious of outsiders; on the other hand, it was quite easy for foreigners to get into Tibet. So, climbers set out from Darjeeling and approached the Himalayas from Tibet. However, at the start of the 1950s all this reversed, with the opening of Nepal's borders and the practically simultaneous closure of Tibet to Westerners after its invasion by the Chinese Communists, who were still in the militant stage of their revolution at that time. Thereafter, Nepal became the go-to place for Himalayan mountaineers and trekkers. The 1953 Everest expedition was one of the very first to approach the Himalayas through Nepalese territory.

The most significant river in all India, the river Ganges, has its source from the snow melt high in the Western Himalaya ranges. The Ganges is culturally and environmentally significant as it is the largest freshwater source in northern India. It is also one of the most sacred sites for Hindu religious practices and burials. Bathing in the Ganges is done for purification and religious rituals. I passed by areas of the Ganges and found a fascinating quality to it. The Ganges has been sacred in Hinduism for many centuries, with a number of individually holy sites along it of which perhaps the best-known worldwide is the city of Varanasi (Benares).

The Valley of Flowers is an Indian national park that is nestled high in the Himalayas. A showcase of rare alpine plants and animals, it is an area that highlights the variety of environments in the Himalayas. The Valley of Flowers is also a common spot for mountaineers and animal lovers. It is home to the Asiatic black bear (found across Asia), one more thing the countries around the Himalayas share.

The Partition of India in 1947 was one of the largest human migrations in history. Today's Pakistan and Bangladesh were carved out of a British India which incorporated the territory of all three modern nations of India, Pakistan, and Bangladesh (part of Pakistan until 1971). Fourteen million Muslims, Sikhs and Hindus had to leave their countries of residence and move either eastward or westward. Sanctioned by the British in their last days as rulers of the Indian sub-continent, the partition was accompanied by mass riots and the killing of hundreds of thousands of people, possibly as many as two million.

One area where the conflict around the time of partition was particularly intense was in the once-autonomous state of Kashmir. The Hindu king who ruled the area, Hari Singh, joined his realm to India on 26 October 1947 even though the area was mostly inhabited by Muslims. This sparked the first Indo-Pakistan War.

In earlier times, the ancient Macedonian-Greek conqueror Alaxander, who is conventionally styled as 'Alexander the Great', invaded both India and northern Pakistan.

Alexander's Macedonian army invaded northern India in 327–326 BCE. He wove his way through the surrounding areas of the Himalayas and the Hindu Kush, including the Indus Valley. Some of his forces stayed behind and founded new cities.

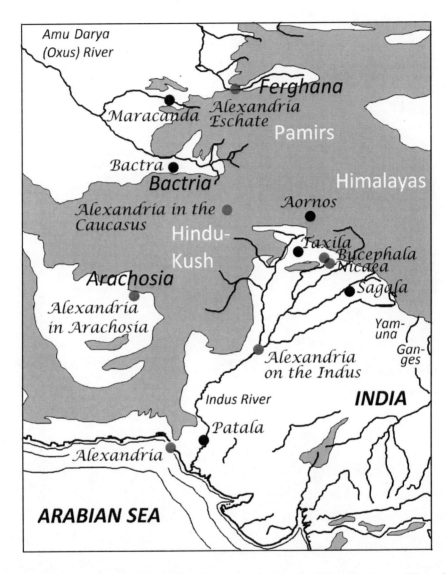

New cities founded by Alexander's forces in and around modern Pakistan. The solid grey denotes mountains. Cities founded by Alexander's forces are shown in grey, alongside older cities in black. The regions have their ancient names.

Another key site I would like to visit in the future is the city of Amritsar. The Golden Temple in Amritsar is a significant temple for Sikhs in the Punjab area. It was near Amritsar where Alexander the Great's army finally began to collapse and be pushed back towards Europe.

Pakistan – Alexander the Great and the Kalash people: I venture alone

Pakistan is officially the Islamic Republic of Pakistan and has a rich history, with interactions and influences stemming as far back as ancient Greece and the Roman Empire.

Pakistan has been ruled and conquered by many different rulers and cultures all influencing the country to be what it is today. There has been a major shift in religious groups within the country since the Partition of India in 1947, when millions of Hindus fled Pakistan to go back to India. Pakistan is unique among Muslim nations as the only one to have been founded specifically as in the name of Islam as such. Although the territory of today's Pakistan was long a Muslim-majority region, the majority is closer to 100% today than in the past. Christians and Hindus combined now make up less than four per cent of the population.

Until 1971, the country known today as Bangladesh was part of Pakistan. Today's Bangladesh was known in those days as East Pakistan, while today's Pakistan was known as West Pakistan. The Muslims of East Pakistan were nearly all ethnically Bengali, a group also widespread in eastern India and in fact one of the most numerous of India's ethnic groups, but not noticeably present in West Pakistan. Comparatively small and dark, the Bengalis looked quite different to the peoples of West Pakistan, who looked more European, and were thus very often the victims of racial discrimination.

These prejudices were little different to those of the British colonisers, who had tended to favour the populations that looked most like themselves, such as the comparatively light-skinned inhabitants of the future West Pakistan. Thus, the independence that came after 1947 was incomplete as far as the inhabitants of East Pakistan were concerned. Now, they were in a colonial dependency of West Pakistan, a country ruled by tall, light-skinned people who had been mates with the British. Or so it appeared to many Bengalis, Hindu and Muslim alike. Religion didn't really come into it.

As such, the union of the Muslims of the east and the west in post-independence Pakistan was literally pious and destined for trouble in the real world. Even if the two parts of the country had been inhabited by the same sorts of people, the great distance between them would still have made the country hard to govern.

East Pakistan finally became independent of the western part of the country after a bloody civil war, in which India intervened.

Since the Partition of India, and the subsequent independence of Bangladesh, there has been a steady decline in people claiming Buddhism, Christianity or Hinduism in Pakistan. Persecution of these groups by extremists and hard-liners has pushed the decline along.

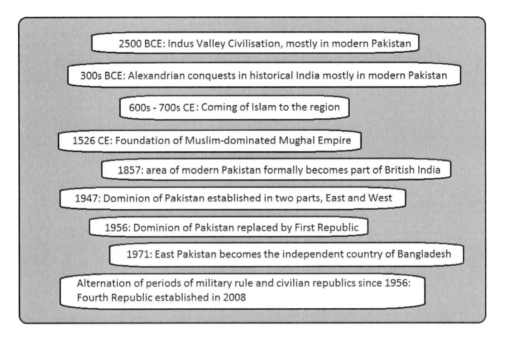

Timeline of the history of Pakistan

Furthermore, despite repeated attempts at homogenisation, there seems to be plenty of evidence of ongoing ethnic and religious tensions within today's Pakistan, including factionalism among its otherwise overwhelming Muslim majority. Bomb explosions and other forms of terrorism are endemic, most of it directed against fellow-Pakistanis held to be of the wrong sort in some way or another.

I found this quite sad, as these amazing countries have such long histories that are intertwined not just for their location under the majestic Himalayas, but also in the development of each culture.

Although Pakistan is no longer divided into West and East, today's Pakistan, the former West Pakistan, still contains a number of distinct ethnic groups, speaking distinct languages of their own in addition to the official language, Urdu, which is similar to India's Hindi but written in an Arabic / Persian script as opposed to Hindi's distinctive Devanagari script.

The four most numerous ethnic groups in today's Pakistan are the Punjabi (of whom many millions also live in India), Pashtun (who are also widespread in Afghanistan), Baloch (who also live in Iran and Afghanistan), and the Sindhi. There are other ethnic groups as well, especially in the more mountainous parts of the country where there are many small minorities. The most numerous groups all live on the plains.

The largest ethno-linguistic group in Pakistan is the Punjabi, to which about 90 million Pakistanis belong, and the smallest is the Kalash, who live in the mountainous Chitral region near Aghanistan's eastern extremity and only number a few thousand.

For a trekker, interacting with mountain minorities such as the Sherpas, and the even less numerous Kalash, can indeed result in a misleading view of the actual ethnic make-up of countries such as Nepal and Pakistan.

Major Ethnic Groups of Pakistan in 1980. Based on a US Central Intelligence Agency colour map which is in the public domain via Wikimedia Commons, itself based on a University of Texas original. For this book, the CIA map has been rendered greyscale and overprinted with the names of the four major ethnic groups in their areas of dominance, in Lucida Calligraphy script.

The Hindu Kush is a significant mountain range in northern Pakistan, which is classed as the western part of the Himalaya chain. The Hindu Kush is only 800 km long but is still a wondrous landscape and terrain. I found this out first-hand when I visited there to do some trails. I stayed with local people and went trekking with a company named Terichmir Travel, run by a man named Abdur Razaq, who I got to know quite well but who was tragically killed on a mountain road in bad weather in 2017.

The people in this area often speak three languages and are just as often well-educated, including the girls; whose education has been put at risk by the Taliban wherever they have managed to take over, of course.

While I was trekking in the Hindu Kush, I met the Kalash, long said to be the lost children of Alexander the Great's army though this isn't scientifically established. Alexander's Macedonian-Greek army invaded northern Pakistan in the fourth century and settled there. Alexander was one of the most significant military commanders of ancient Greece. His lands stretched from as far east as the Punjab in India, via Persia, which is the old name for modern-day Iran.

The Macedonian Empire that Alexander created was vast and widespread, bringing his armies into direct contact with people of Asia and the Middle East. He ruled what is now Iraq and Kurdistan after the Macedonian Army's victory in 331 BCE at the Battle of Gaugamela. There is apparently even a mention of Alexander in the Qur'an (strictly, Qur'ān) – historians believe that the story of Dhu al-Qarnayn may be a reference to Alexander.

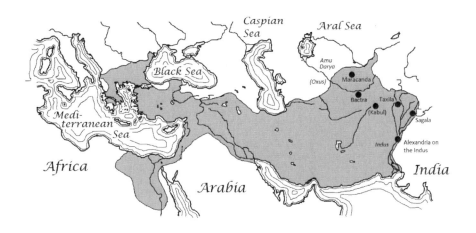

Map of the Empire of Alexander the Great 334–323 BCE

There are many areas of cultural significance that show how diverse the area has long been. The ruins of a Buddhist monastery established in the first century sit in the hilly and rocky area of Takht-i-Bahi. It is one of the most well-preserved examples of Pakistani Buddhist history. Another area of cultural significance is Thatta, where structures built by the Muslim Mughal empire lie within the older Makli complex of monuments, which includes a necropolis.

There was a surprisingly large Greek influence in India and central Asia during the centuries after Alexander, centred on such areas as Bactria, comprising the Ferghana Valley in modern Uzbekistan, Kyrgyzstan and Tajikistan, along with parts of modern Afghanistan and northern Pakistan, and also extending into India proper. (It's after Bactria that the two-humped Bactrian camel is named.)

Greek culture was even influential on Buddhism, at that time still a primarily Indian religion, lately extended into Bactria. It seems to have been the Greeks who first persuaded the Buddhists that making images of the Buddha would not be disrespectful or vain. The realistic statutes of the Buddha that were erected all over Asia during the subsequent Buddhist diaspora often include specifically Greek-invented features, such as skilfully carved representations of draped togas ('himation', after the Greek word for toga).

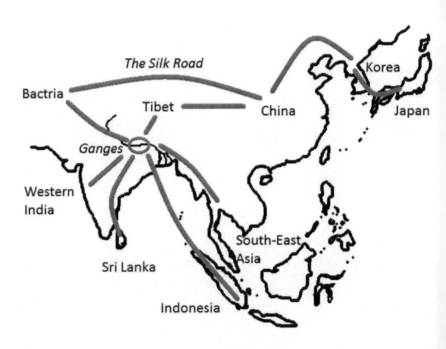

The diffusion of Buddhism in Asia, from its origin in the Ganges Plain. Graphic based on multiple sources.

Here are photos of two sides of a coin minted by the Kushan, that is to say, Bactrian, Emperor Kanishka I, a Buddhist ruler who reigned from approximately 127-150 CE from a city known then as Purusapura and today as Peshawar, in Pakistan. The writing on the coin is in a local form of the Greek alphabet. On one side there is an image of the emperor styling himself as 'shaonashao' or 'King of Kings' in the Persian fashion, just like the last Shah of Iran in the 1970s. On the other side is an image of the Buddha in the flowing robes of classical statuary beside a caption reading BODDO, which requires no translation!

Coin of Kanishka I. Images made available by the Classical Numismatic Group, Inc, URL www.cngcoins.com, CC BY-SA 3.0.

So, there seems to have been a bit of everything in the central Asian kingdoms of that era. They displayed a hybrid vigour, which contains real lessons for those preoccupied with notions of cultural purity. The famous line that East is East, and West is West, and the two will never meet, is simply nonsense.

The central Asian melting-pot explains why a Japanese Buddha today is draped in a similar fashion to a statue of Julius Caesar or Cicero.

I find it just fascinating the hundreds of connections we have to each other: many we just simply do not know about or are lost in the overlapping histories.

More about The Silk Road

My map of the diffusion of Buddhism shows a part of the Silk Road. The Silk Road was a series of trading routes that brought with it easier ways to share ideas and religions, extending for thousands of kilometres across China, India and central Asia into the Middle East, the Mediterranean, and parts of Africa. Antioch, once of the most important cities of the classical Mediterranean, located just north of Syria in the modern Turkish provinces of Hatay (itself once part of Syria), was the Western terminus of the part of the Silk Road that ran through Persia. Another branch of the Silk Road extended southward to seaports on what is now the coast of Pakistan, for goods that were destined for the Red Sea and the cities of Egypt.

Buddhism, amongst other religions, was carried by traders and other travellers who followed the Silk Road east to China. The Silk Road developed during the Chinese Han Dynasty and was already fully established by the time of the Caesars. The Silk Road became not only a historically significant means of trade for economies but also for cultural ideas. The sharing of ideas, philosophies and religions made the Silk Road one of the most important means of communication in the ancient world. The Chinese government is currently investing in transport infrastructure that it terms the 'New Silk Road'.

These days, the Silk Road is also metaphor for East-West interaction. The metaphor is, of course, based in solid reality, as solid as the coins of Kanishka.

I have discussed my pilgrim walks across Europe in my book *A Maverick Pilgrim Way*, which describes my love of discovery and exploration of historical trails. In fact, there are many pilgrim trails in and around the Himalayas created by conquerors, invaders, missionaries and trade routes – but that's a story for another book!

I suppose we all like to think we are so very different, and in some respects we are. But if we look closer, we can see great similarities as well – we are not so different after all.

Website version of this chapter:

a-maverick.com/blog/himalayan-history

CHAPTER TWO

Arriving in Nepal

I follow the path of famous mountaineers to Nepal — and discover Kathmandu!

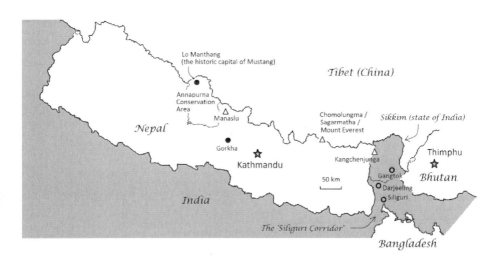

Nepal and its immediate neighbours. India is shown as grey.

LIKE most Kiwis, I grew up on stories of our celebrated mountaineer and humanitarian, Sir Edmund Hillary, who together with Tenzing Norgay was first to summit the mountain we all knew as Everest in 1953. I pored over his books and read his autobiography *Nothing Venture, Nothing Win* several times. In the foreword he writes, "I discovered that even the mediocre can have adventures and even the fearful can achieve." He repeatedly emphasised his humble origins and the fact that anyone, even those with mediocre talents, can achieve

39

a lot if they drive themselves. "You don't have to be a fantastic hero to do certain things – to compete. You can be just an ordinary chap, sufficiently motivated to take challenging goals," Sir Ed told his interviewers. I thought about his 1953 conquest of Mt Everest with primitive mountaineering equipment by today's standards, and the challenges he must have encountered.

Well, I too could make it, step by step. First step: Nepal's Everest Base Camp.

People sometimes refer to this camp as the Nepalese or Southern Base Camp for Mount Everest, as there is also a base camp in Tibet for the few who try Everest's northern faces. However, I don't go into Tibet in any of the travels in this book. So, I will just generally refer to the camp as Everest Base Camp, or Base Camp if it is obvious which mountain I'm referring to.

I was drawn to Mount Everest, known to the Tibetans as Chomolungma and in Sanskrit, the ancient Hindu liturgical language of India and Nepal, as Sagarmatha, or more correctly as Sagarmāthā, not only because of its beauty but because of all the other mountains that surrounded it as well. All of them fascinated me. It was as if everywhere you looked were mountains.

My training began at the Auckland Tramping Club. What did I expect? After nine hours of presentations, I was prepared for yak poo, dust and small bowls of water to wash myself. Not exactly a great first impression. The Auckland Tramping Club members who had been to the Everest Base Camp had stayed in tents and done it the hard way, with some of them suffering from altitude sickness. One guy I met had shown me his blackened hands from frostbite after a failed attempt to climb Mt Everest from the Chinese side. He thought that would have been an easier route.

I had registered with Trek and Tours, a Nepalese-owned adventure company, and received their itinerary. The trek itself was a total of thirteen days, but they had also included sightseeing trips in Kathmandu. We were to stay in tea houses along the trail, which I was quite happy with.

It was my first time in a country with such high mountains and I liked the idea of being on a guided trip with a team of twenty people. It was a gentle introduction.

The tramping club presentations recommended that people take care to acclimatise slowly to the altitude. It was important to let your body take the time to adjust to thinner air. Some people arrived in Kathmandu, which is at an altitude of 1,400 metres or 4,600 feet above sea level and would only then stay one night before flying to Lukla at 2,860 metres or 9,380 feet, thus gaining altitude far too quickly for the body to adapt.

Not letting yourself acclimatise can lead to serious problems, like blood clots in the brain. Why would people risk it?

My loyal travel companion was my medical kit. I normally stay away from medicines (even Diamox, which is used for altitude sickness) but altitude sickness can be a killer and I didn't want to be sick in Nepal.

EBC BASE CAMP TREK 2014-GRPA

TOUR/TREK CODE: EBC31MAR2014

DATE	DAYS	ITINERARY
31 Mar	01	Arrive in Kathmandu or meet our representative in Kathmandu Airport – transfer to hotel. 05:00PM: Briefing at the Hotel Lobby (Requested everyone to be at the hotel Lobby) O/N Marshyangdi.
01 Apr	02	Breakfast at the hotel. 09.30AM: Pick up from the Hotel Lobby & Depart for sightseeing tour Sightseeing tour of Patan, Patan Durbar Square Lunch at Boudha – Boudha Kitchen on your own. After Lunch sightseeing tour of Boudhnath and Swayambhunath (Monkey Temple O/N Marshyangdi.
02 Apr	03	Breakfast at the hotel 04:45 AM: Pickup from hotel and transfer to airport. 06.15 AM: Fly to Lukla (2,795 m) and trek to Phakding (2,610m) O/N Lodge.
03 Apr	04	Trek to Namche Bazaar (3,480m). O/N Lodge.
04 Apr	05	Acclimatization day in Namche. O/ N Lodge.
05 Apr	06	Trek to Tengboche Monastery (3,860m). O/N Lodge.
06 Apr	07	Trek to Dingboche (4,350m). O/N Lodge.
07 Apr	08	Day trip to Chhukung valley (4,710m) and return trek to Dingboche. O/N Lodge.
08 Apr	09	Trek to Lobuche (4,920m). O/N Lodge.
09 Apr	10	Trek to Everest Base Camp (5,300m), then back to Gorak Shep. O/N Lodge.
10 Apr	11	Visit Kalapattar (5,545m), and trek to Pheriche (4,240m). O/N Lodge.
11 Apr	12	Trek Khumjung (3,790m). O/N Lodge.
12 Apr	13	Trek to Monjo (2,840m). O/N Lodge.
13 Apr	14	Trek to Lukla (2,795m). O/N Lodge.
14 Apr	15	07.00AM: Lukla/Kathmandu flight. Free time to relax. O/N Marshyangdi.
15 Apr	16	Breakfast at the hotel. Kathmandu – Time on your own - sightseeing can be arranged. 06.30 PM: Pick up from the hotel lobby and transfer for farewell dinner. After dinner transfer to hotel. O/N Marshyangdi.
16 Apr	17	Breakfast at the hotel Last day of trip – transfer to International airport for departure.

~END OF A MEMORABLE TRIP~

My travel itinerary to Base Camp and back

To avoid intestinal problems, I also became a struggling vegetarian for the duration of the trip. My drug kit contained the diarrhoea stopper loperamide, some ciprofloxacin antibiotics, packets of Gastrolyte rehydration solution, Tramadol, Tiger Balm, Vaseline for dry skin, tea tree oil, iodine and bandages, and, finally, plain old paracetamol. Not exactly a romantic set-up, but realistic, nonetheless. Someone joked that I would probably be able to walk out if I had a broken leg!

Flying to Nepal and meeting Kiwi mountaineer Lydia Bradey

We left for Nepal via Hong Kong on Malaysia Airlines flight MH370. This was quite unnerving given the disappearance of another MH370 flight earlier that month. A more improbable coincidence awaited as I was transiting at the Hong Kong airport. I ran into Lydia Bradey, a New Zealand mountaineer who summited Mt Everest in 1988 at the age of 27 without oxygen or a permit. In fact, she's the first woman to ever climb Everest without supplemental oxygen. I had heard her being interviewed on New Zealand National Radio.

Because of the lack of a permit, Bradey's achievement was denied by her team-mates Rob Hall and Gary Ball, a denial which Bradey herself reluctantly went along with for a while and has only recently been acknowledged. I've included a link to a 2013 media story at the end of this chapter. In 2015, Penguin Books published an autobiography by Lydia Bradey with Laurence Fearnley. It's called *Lydia Bradey: Going Up is Easy*. I've read the book; it's tragic that her feat was not recognised until the last decade. Her ascent of Everest and subsequent falling-out with team-mates Hall and Ball and the New Zealand mountain-climbing establishment is covered from Chapter 12 onwards in that book.

That afternoon, I was surprised to see Lydia at the Hong Kong Airport. A friend of hers, Nick, had previously done a High Alpine Skills Course with me on Aoraki/Mt Cook in New Zealand, and had told me about her. I was in the departure lounge, and she approached me and asked me if she could borrow my *Sunday Star-Times*. I gave it to her and asked if she was Lydia Bradey. She was very surprised and asked me how I recognised her. I told her she was a friend of a friend and that I had heard her on New Zealand National Radio. I also said that it was dreadful that it had taken so long for her to be recognised for summiting Mt Everest without oxygen. We also talked about my plans for a trek in Pakistan with Patricia Deavoll, another leading New Zealand mountaineer. Lydia told me she had recently been to the capital city Islamabad with Patricia, and that they had witnessed bombs exploding, but she assured me that I would be safe while in the Himalayan districts of Pakistan.

Kathmandu – No traffic lights in a city of millions. They stop for cows.

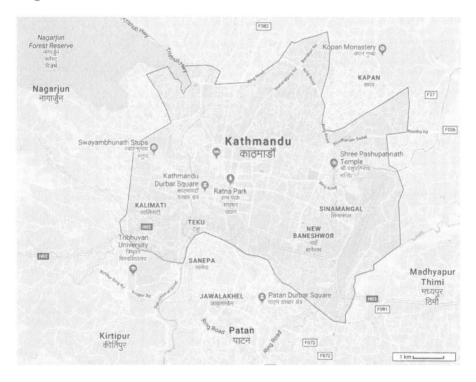

Kathmandu and Patan (Lalitpur). This map shows the location of Swayambhunath, Kathmandu Durbar Square, and Patan Durbar Square. Map data ©2018 Google

At Kathmandu's Tribhuvan International Airport, the disorganisation was overwhelming. There were people everywhere loaded up with hiking and mountaineering gear. It was a small airport, not big enough to support the huge crowds arriving to climb mountains or whatever else they were there for. There were only two conveyor belts in the airport which would every now and then just stop and then a few minutes later start up again loaded up with luggage. If you needed to weigh your luggage, they had some ancient-looking scales. I thought that was quite funny. Out the front of the airport there were rickshaws everywhere! (Recently, the airport has been upgraded to six baggage conveyors; progress marches on.)

After we eventually got out of the airport, we were ushered into a bus for a long ride into the city. The fumes from the road were unbearable; carbon monoxide and carbon dioxide – a choice between sweltering heat with the windows closed or having the windows open and being poisoned! Not a choice, really. Pedestrians wore masks to protect themselves from the fumes. I also noticed that Kathmandu seemed to be full of knockoffs of North Face and other Western labels. You find them across the city. I preferred to buy Nepalese-made brands which are original and last longer. Sometimes it pays not to be hip. I bought shirts, trousers, gloves and hats made from yak wool there: a very famous product.

Trekkers in Nepal can go freely in many areas as a 'Free Individual Trekker' or FIT, or as an informal group. However, in parts of Nepal known as Restricted Areas, trekkers (and climbers) must travel in formal groups, with permits and guides. In general, the Restricted Areas are the more elevated, dangerous and ecologically or culturally sensitive areas. Many of the permits are quite cheap and seem to be aimed at ensuring group safety, though for a few exotic areas such as Upper Mustang, an isolated Himalayan kingdom-within-a-kingdom until 2008, the charge is quite steep and presumably aimed at limiting tourism's impact.

It was my first visit to Kathmandu. The capital city has a total population of three million, out of Nepal's total population of 29 million people. The roads were gloriously chaotic, with no traffic lights to maintain order. Power blackouts were a fact of life, and people had solar power panels hooked up everywhere. Even a small solar setup was useful for keeping things like wifi alive and charging mobile phones through blackouts, which were quite frequent.

We stayed in an area in the inner city called Thamel, a popular area where all the tourists and travellers stayed. The guiding companies and eateries were there too, and you could see tours advertised on big boards, expeditions to climb Mount Mera and every possible place you could go, along with massages for the hikers and mannequins dressed in all the latest gear outside shops that sold the same.

The streets were thin, dirt-lined paths, so narrow I don't know how anyone managed to get down them in a truck. All the streets were lined with shops; there were shops with wooden knick-knacks, yak clothing shops, shops with hats and gloves – everything was woollen – jewellery shops and hiking shops. It was quite marvellous how they crammed so much into the tiny streets, which were alive with commerce.

I got a chance to get out and have a wander around. Everywhere you looked wires were just jumbled together and hanging off buildings or across streets. Some hung so low you could have caught your head on one. 'Om' chants blasting from the sound systems of stores selling Buddhist mandalas and other religious artwork could be heard everywhere. There were Buddhist shrines and Hindu shrines on every street corner, and sometimes it was hard for a traveller to tell the difference.

Kathmandu: Tangle of Wires, and Buddhist Monks

Kathmandu Street Life with temples

Kathmandu

Kathmandu

Monkey Statue in the Golden Temple, Kathmandu

Everest Base Camp Trekking Party, Kathmandu. The author is second from left.

Electric power cuts were so common there that the locals didn't bat an eyelid when they happened. The power would go out any time of the day without any warning! I found out that most of the factories only operated from one a.m. to seven a.m. because most of the people were asleep then; that was the time when power supplies were most reliable. I was also told by my guide that India owned the power companies, as strange as that is.

Boudhanath, Swayambunath and Lalitpur (Patan)

We visited Lalitpur, historically known as Patan, an ancient royal city known for its Durbar square, a combination of temples and palaces. Lalitpur is located just across the Bagmati River from Kathmandu and is effectively a suburb of greater Kathmandu these days.

Taking a roundabout and scenic route to Lalitpur from downtown Kathmandu, we visited the ancient Buddhist stupas of Boudhanath and Charumati, which feature painted eyes that represent the all-seeing nature of Buddha. Although Nepal is over 80% Hindu, Boudhanath is perhaps the most recognizable of Nepal's heritage buildings to outsiders, in view of its striking appearance.

The word 'stupa' literally means mound or heap; a stupa resembles an old-fashioned burial mound of the kind heaped up in many cultures, and is erected over a sacred Buddhist relic, as a place of meditation.

Around Boudhanath, I saw more shops that sold mandalas and other Buddhist symbols, and taught students the art of painting them as well. We also went to Swayambhunath (the Monkey Temple). It was one of many fascinating Tibetan Buddhist sites, and was an amazing area to visit.

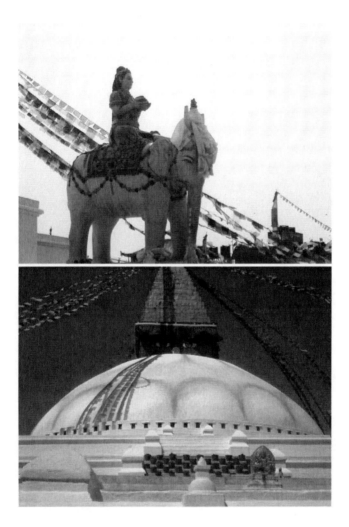

White elephant statue at Boudhanath (top), and Boudhanath Stupa (below)

The Charumati Stupa ('Little Boudhanath'), and Buddha statues at Swayambunath Temple, Kathmandu

Air pollution sunset at Swayambunath Temple, Kathmandu

The Shankar Narayan Mandir in Patan Durbar Square, destroyed in the April 2015 earthquake

A lion guarding the Krishna Mandir (temple)

The Boudhanath Stupa lost its golden steeple for a time as a result of the disastrous April 2015 earthquake, which killed 9,000 people and inflicted great damage to Nepal's architectural heritage as well. The earthquake happened after I was on this tour; it destroyed many old temples in the Kathmandu Valley, including an ancient temple called the Kasthamandap that predated the Norman conquest of England (!) and gave Kathmandu its name.

Fortunately, many other historic temples and other ancient buildings survived or suffered only easily repairable damage, including the Krishna Mandir, probably the most finely worked

58

stone temple in all Lalitpur. David Ways has an excellent, illustrated 'Guide to Temples and Buildings Destroyed in the 2015 Earthquake', on his website, **thelongestwayhome.com**.

Website version of this chapter

a-maverick.com/blog/arriving-in-nepal

References about Lydia Bradey

Easily accessed online: Michael Daly, 'Everest's history marked in blood', 29 May 2013, stuff.co.nz/world/8729630/Everests-history-marked-in-blood. Not so easily accessed online: In addition to *Lydia Bradey: Going Up is Easy,* see also Nicola Russell, 'Reaching Great Heights', *New Zealand Women's Weekly*, 15 July 2015.

CHAPTER THREE

Flying Into the Mountains

Soon you'll be able to drive there, but it won't be as much fun!

THAT evening, we met the team and the guides for the trek. There were twenty of us in the group with five lead guides from the trek company, Karma Sherpa and Gyalzen Sherpa, and their assistants, Pemba Sherpa, Jeta Tamang Sherpa and Dawa Sherpa. There were also ten Sherpa porters whose name I didn't know.

The group comprised Aussies and Kiwis and there was a good mixture of ages, with both young and old people. This meant we would bond well and help each other out if someone was sick.

The trek company checked the bags we were carrying. We were allowed a single duffel bag with all our clothes and a day bag with our immediate requirements, and together they had to weigh no more than 14 kg. It was amazing what I got in my bag: two trousers, four shirts, Birkenstock sandals, spare walking shoes, water purifier, two long-sleeved shirts, a down jacket, a fleece jacket, a sleeping bag, a thermal liner and of course, my medical kit!

After breakfast at the hotel, we left Kathmandu and flew to Lukla from where we would begin our first day's trek to Phakding, a small village at an altitude of 2,610 metres. Upon landing at Lukla's Tenzing-Hillary Airport, we were immediately surrounded by porters who were waiting for work.

Lukla's airport was officially named Tenzing-Hillary in 2008, the year of the famously modest Sir Edmund Hillary's death (Tenzing, an Indian citizen who was never knighted, had died in 1986). The airport had been built at the instigation of Sir Edmund, who envisioned its use as a way of bringing in supplies every now and then, and not as a major tourist airport. The runway is short and steeply sloping, with hills at one end and a precipice at the other. The effect is a bit like landing on an aircraft carrier, with the upward slope of the runway acting as an arrester on landing and the downward slope as a catapult on takeoff. This is all the more necessary as, at over 9,000 feet, the air under the wings is thin, and engine power not what it would be at sea level.

A lot of mountain airstrips used by hill-country farmers, deer-hunters and the like have the same squeezed-in design as Tenzing-Hillary; but it's a bit hard-case for a passenger airport.

In fact, these days, Tenzing-Hillary is rated the world's most dangerous airport by some authorities. There have been many takeoff and landing accidents a Tenzing-Hillary over the years, though with surprisingly few of them fatal; perhaps because only expert pilots, piloting special bush aircraft designed for short strips, are allowed to attempt Lukla in the first place.

(The terrible accident that claimed Hillary's wife and daughter in 1975 was at the nearby airport of Phaplu on the other side of the Dudh Kosi Valley; a supposedly safer airport, but a plane flown by a less expert pilot.)

To make matters worse, Lukla's airstrip is often socked in by mountain weather for days on end. In the days when it was only used for freight this was no big deal. And even in the 1970s the few hardy souls who chartered a plane to get to Lukla in preference to hiking in for a week from the town of Jiri near Kathmandu, as Hillary and Tenzing had done in 1953, were generally philosophical about the vagaries of mountain weather.

They say that the old 1950s expedition route through the Himalayan foothills from Jiri is very scenic. A few people still do it, but 95% of visitors to the Everest region currently fly into Lukla via Tenzing-Hillary airport.

But by the same token this means that Hillary's old bush airstrip now accepts 30,000 arrivals a year, many of them the sorts of people who got impatient if the planes were delayed by bad weather. In 2011 they were delayed for six days. That's a long time to be staring out the window at the rain coming down, especially if you are booked on ahead.

In the age of modern mass tourism, Tenzing-Hillary was becoming a relic of the bush pilot era, no longer fit for purpose.

Fortunately, a good-quality road to Lukla has been under construction for several years and now reaches past Phaplu, in various stages of surfacing. The plan is that the road will soon be sealed all the way to Lukla, and the climbers and trekkers will then be able to catch a bus from Kathmandu.

Then again, how unromantic! The fabled white-knuckle destination of Lukla will be just like everywhere else once the road is completed, and especially so if the Tenzing-Hillary airport is decommissioned in favour of asphalt, buses and Phaplu.

You can't stop progress, rationally speaking. All the same, I predict that if the alternative becomes sealed roads, tourist coaches and a normal sort of an airport, the old expedition route will undergo a trekking revival!

Boarding the plane to Lukla, at Kathmandu

Lukla, from the airport with a view of Mount Khumbila

Website version of this chapter

a-maverick.com/blog/flying-into-the-mountains

CHAPTER FOUR

Everest Base Camp

Learning to share the track with yaks – and dzos, mules, porters, guides, mountaineers, trekkers and horses!

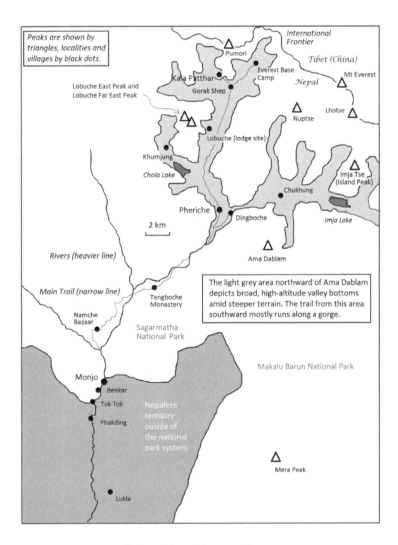

Everest Base Camp trek map

ON our way to from Lukla to Phakding, we shared the path with yaks carrying 60 kg loads, mules with lovely decorations and lots of puppies and dogs. The landscape was dotted with teahouses where you could get a bed for the night. You could also buy fried rice for $2 and lots of honey tea with ginger. The view of the peaks was amazing, and there were magnolia trees and rhododendrons in bloom, all laden with the blossoms of spring.

Hill country farms near Lukla

Dzos. These are hybrids of yaks and domestic cattle, often used as beasts of burden in a similar fashion to mules.

Loading up a Mule

Pack animals crossing a bridge near Namche Bazaar

Dzos, and Village Snowfall

Setting out on the Everest Base Camp Trek

Karma's Sunwise Mills

Every village we passed through had a stupa with the painted eyes of Buddha as well as prayer wheels decorated with ancient Tibetan mantras.

The phrase prayer wheel is a misnomer: 'mantra mill' of 'mill of good karma' (positive spiritual energy) would be more accurate. The words on the so-called prayer wheels, which are in fact cylindrical, are not lengthy prayers but short repetitive mantras that would normally be repeated or chanted. Whoever spins the prayer wheel may as well have chanted the mantras for as long as it keeps spinning.

Some prayer wheels are kept in motion by water wheels, some by wind (when it blows), some by rising hot air from flames (a gas turbine, technically speaking) and some, today, by electricity. These spiritual mills come in many sizes and degrees of sophistication, from serried banks of large ones at the most important monasteries to small hand-held ones that are operated individually and by hand.

And that's another reason to call a prayer wheel a mantra mill. It's a device by which Tibetan Buddhism industrialised the production of chants that would bring them good karma. The parallels include the search for sources of power and realisation that something endlessly spinning was the most efficient producer.

It really is a valid parallel to the Industrial Revolution. You automate or industrialise the spinning of whatever you think is a really important substance. For nineteenth-century Britons it was cotton; and for Tibetan Buddhism it is the good karma of the religious chant.

The mills of good karma must always rotate clockwise as viewed from above or from the eye of the beholder, since anticlockwise is regarded as the evil direction just as it traditionally was in the West. For instance, before clocks were invented, the British called the anticlockwise direction widdershins: a word with all sorts of spooky connotations.

Some say widdershins means 'opposite sense', a cognate of German *widersinnig*. But I prefer the other possibility that it literally meant against the sun (*sin* in old Scots) or against the light, *wider Schein* in German. This seems just as likely, since the clockwise direction used to be called 'sunwise', the way the sun moved around a sundial in the Northern Hemisphere.

Anyhow, if you should come across fairies dancing in circles at the onset of twilight, you should hope that they are dancing sunwise, not widdershins.

A Tibetan-Buddhist prayer wheel spinning against the light or anti-sunwise, if that's what the other direction means, would thus grind out negative energy and darkness: a bit like a vinyl record played backwards by black-clad heavy-metallers back hoping to hear the voice of Satan, I suppose!

For, twentieth-century gramophone records obeyed the sunwise rule too. And CDs and DVDs, even in the modern electronic age. Most probably the hard drive hidden away inside in my computer also spins sunwise as viewed from above. I'm starting to hope so, now!

There's another parallel to my hard disk, by the way. Along with the messages on the outside, prayer wheels are often filled with pieces of paper on which additional mantras are written. That's the main reason for the large size and drum-like shape of public prayer wheels. These are not just mills of karma, but karma drives.

I was told never to stop a correctly rotating prayer wheel. At a minimum, I would be robbing whoever had set it in motion of their rightful reward of good karma from the mill. And no doubt, I would probably get an electric-shock dose of the bad stuff too.

Phakding to Namche Bazaar – First glimpse at 3,000 metres

The next morning, we were preparing to set out for Namche Bazaar, but many people in the group were down with a fever. We shared our medication and wished them all the best. We were to climb to 3,480 metres that day, giving ourselves a further day to acclimatise to the altitude in Namche Bazaar once we arrived. The morning was sunny after an early start at 4.30 a.m. Breakfast was porridge and an apple. We walked slowly, taking in the beauty all around us. There was a great view of Thamserku Mountain.

The walk was straight uphill to Namche Bazaar, with steep cliffs that dropped away on either side of the trail. Namche Bazaar is a small town which is an important stop for climbers, as they stop for a while before continuing higher into their ascent.

People go to Everest for all kinds of reasons. Some on the group had not done any hiking or training in their home countries to get fit. In fact, one man did not even have boots that fitted him properly. This man and his wife were recovering from a very tragic episode in their lives. Their son had become brain-damaged at the age of 29 from a mysterious illness. Until a year ago they were his caregivers, but they couldn't cope any longer and decided to put him in a home. I felt immense respect for this couple when I heard their story. They came down with the flu on the trip and I was surprised this was all they came down with given their lack of preparation. We also had an Australian nurse in our group who must have had over 200 tablets of Diamox which she distributed very freely. Her generosity was marvellous.

There are lots of wire suspension bridges on the trail, including a very high and scary one officially known as the Sir Edmund Hillary Bridge. If you are coming from Phakding, this bridge is the last bridge to cross before you get to Namche Bazaar: with about another two hours' walk ahead before you get to the town.

The high bridge was erected a few years ago, above a now-decaying bridge built, I believe, in the 1960s with the help of Sir Edmund Hillary, and also known as the Sir Edmund Hillary Bridge in its day.

The old bridge is still there. But I don't think anyone is supposed to use it now.

The trail and its bridges are used both by trekkers and porters, and also by local people moving goods on yaks, dzos and mules. The resulting traffic jams can get dangerous given that the trail and its bridges aren't very wide.

Trekking slowly, we came to the Sir Edmund Hillary Bridge. It looked like the bridge could take only eight to ten mules carrying heavy loads. It scared me when there were forty people on the bridge, not to mention the mules and the more massive yaks and dzos also bearing heavy loads. After three attempts, I managed to get across! It snowed that day which provided a beautiful first view of the Himalayas.

We made it to Namche Bazaar where we dined on *dal bhat*. Dal bhat is the Nepali national food consisting of curried potato and lentil soup with rice. If you were hungry, you could get second or third helpings.

During the acclimatisation day, we ascended another 400 metres to the Sagarmāthā National Park, a protected area with a rugged terrain cut by deep rivers and glaciers. Sagarmāthā, the Sanskrit name, comes from *sagar* meaning sky and *māthā* meaning head or forehead, and is also the everyday Nepali-language name for Mt Everest.

The Tibetans and their Sherpa relatives call the mountain Chomolungma, or Chomolangma, meaning mother goddess of the Earth.

Photos at Sagarmāthā National Park headquarters

Established in 1972, Sagarmāthā National Park was an initiative of Sir Edmund Hillary. It covers an area of 1,148 square kilometres, and over the years it has been the site of an afforestation project as well. We had great views of the

79

mountains of Lhotse, Ama Dablam and Kusum Kanguru from the park, but we were still waiting for our first sight of Mt Everest.

There was a great museum at Namche Bazaar. They had information and exhibits about the Sherpa people and rhododendrons (which are native to the region and are the national flower of Nepal), and information about the decline in numbers of snow leopards and bears. I also learnt that people were chopping down wood for fuel in the park, with deforestation becoming a real issue.

Namche Bazaar Museum: old photos of traditional eye protection against snowblindness, a bit like the traditional googles used for the same purpose in the Arctic

All kitted up at Namche Bazaar, and ready to go!

I finally got a view of Everest that day: a great view. I decided to celebrate. I gave up my less-than-a-week-vegetarian status and enjoyed some chicken curry – yum! The local farmers were fertilising their fields and planting out potatoes and bok choy for the spring. There were crows plucking hair off cows for their nests. Some teahouses we visited had no mains power, but all the teahouses used solar energy: conservation of power was a must. I went to an outdoor market and there were so many bakeries with delicious smells wafting around. There were a few people stocking up on hiking items, as Namche Bazaar is the last town on the trail where you can purchase tents and gear.

By this time, some of our group members had developed altitude sickness and were taking Diamox. Others had chest infections.

Namche Bazaar to Tengboche and Dingboche – The highest bakery in the world and meditation at 6 a.m.

We left Namche Bazaar for Tengboche Monastery, which is at 3,860 metres. The day was overcast and the ascent gradual. For the first time we saw yaks, as they do not live below this altitude. They looked like hairy cows and had bells around their necks. They are worth $500 each, and their owners were known to be wealthy by local standards.

Tengboche was a beautiful town full of craftspeople, with a famous, lavishly decorated Buddhist monastery. I saw people making windows and a new house for the monks, as well as the highest bakery in the world. The next morning, we rose to attend a seven-a.m. meditation service in the monastery. It was really cold outside the monastery gates, with beautiful views of Mt Everest and Ama Dablam. Twenty people went in, and the monks burnt incense, chanted and banged drums for thirty minutes. There was beautiful, fantastically detailed decoration with many images of religious scenes and different Buddhas (for there are many Buddhas, though Gautama is the one usually meant), and other spiritual beings.

Stupa in front of Ama Dablam

Trekking toward Ama Dablam

At Tengboche

At Tengboche Monastery

The Buddha resisting temptation by a demon in the form of a beautiful woman: a famous story, akin to the temptation of Christ. Three such demons threw themselves at the Buddha, egged on by their father, an even worse demon named Mara; but the Buddha managed to wrestle himself free of the embrace of all three. Although such demons are known in Christendom in the form of succubi, *so explicit a depiction of their assaults probably wouldn't be considered appropriate for the walls of a European monastery! The Buddha's hand gesture (mudra) has a special significance here, possibly warding off evil.*

At the time, two films were being made about the Sherpas – one was a British production and the other by a New Zealand filmmaker. Dzos and porters were carrying loads of equipment that looked like they weighed at least 60 kg. A voluntary code of

35 kg was meant to be implemented, but this was often ignored. International film crews should have known better. By 8.00 a.m. the next morning, we had beautiful views of Mt Everest and Ama Dablam, but as we climbed to Dingboche, the next village at a height of 4,410 metres, the weather closed in. By the time we reached Shomare, halfway along our day's journey, the visibility dropped rapidly, and we needed our snow gear. People in our group were suffering from altitude sickness, and some were shaking and going from feeling hot to feeling cold.

That night I went to bed early. Altitude sickness is a very deceptive illness. For reading, I had brought Jon Krakauer's *Into Thin Air,* a book based on his 1996 expedition to the Everest in which eight climbers were killed and many stranded following a storm. In a little more detail, *Into Thin Air* is a non-fiction book about how Rob Hall, a climbing guide with the New Zealand company Adventure Consultants, perished on Everest in 1996 along with four others. Krakauer is an American, who was a member of the New Zealand-led climbing team. Krakauer blamed the Russian guide, Anatoli Boukreev, for the disaster. For his part, Boukreev, who was killed on Annapurna on Christmas Day, 1997, also co-wrote a book rebutting such claims. Just after I finished my own trek to Everest Base Camp, fourteen Sherpa had perished on Everest in an avalanche at the Khumbu Icefall.

(I give full references for both books at the end of this chapter.)

In *Into Thin Air,* Krakauer also mentions how both Sherpas and Western climbers can be in denial about altitude sickness, which can lead to them endangering expeditions and, ultimately, dying.

There are two main medical causes of death in the mountains, altitude sickness and heart attacks. Blood clots are another one that has been the cause of numerous deaths and failed attempts to ascend Mt Everest.

Dingboche

In front of Ama Dablam

Imja Tse (Island Peak)

Solar Cookers

Daytrip to Chukhung Valley – Views of Everest ever closer!

On the way out from Tengboche, there were beautiful magnolias. The trek to the Chukhung Valley was part of our acclimatisation. We climbed 400 metres and had great views of Ama Dablam's southwest face as well as Imja Tse (Island Peak), Lhotse and views of glaciers by what the locals called the Holy Mountain. This was at 4,730 metres. Many in the group had by now acquired puffy faces from the high altitude and had to take Diamox. I learnt that locals have to leave town throughout June and July as the mountain authorities require that they leave. We returned and stayed the night at Dingboche.

Camouflaged rock bird

Gorak Shep / 'shit' – The worst toilet in the world

On our way to Everest Base Camp, we paused at Gorak Shep where we would return to spend the night on the way back from Base Camp. It took five hours to reach Gorak Shep where we were welcomed by an overflowing toilet! It oozed and overflowed everywhere. Apparently, the problem was longstanding and trekkers called the place Gorak Shit. Maybe it's been fixed since then. I hope so.

After lunch we trekked on towards Everest Base Camp alongside big rocks and boulders. The views were divine: mountains everywhere! I almost felt drunk from the views.

Gorak Shep was a monumental stop for me as it was the original site of Sir Edmund Hillary's base camp. Due to changes in the landscape, melting of glaciers and global warming, it had to be moved to its current position higher up the mountain.

It was a long day, with an eight-hour ascent, but it was a truly beautiful day for the climb. There was ice all over the trail and you had to be careful not to slip. You had to watch every step you took, as there were crevasses to the side and it would be so easy to slip and fall in, never to be seen again. Surprisingly, there was quite a bit of traffic on the trail! We had to dodge mules and yaks and dzos loaded with supplies and other people coming back down the mountain. I remembered the complaints about 'yak poo' everywhere, and, well, they were right. If it wasn't mule poo on the trail, then it was yak or dzo, and it was everywhere! The yaks and dzos were carrying food to other climbers or going down to the nearest town to find more. It could get very crowded in places, especially along the narrower sections of the trail. You could hear the yaks and dzos coming, as they had bells on their collars, and the lilting jingle became very familiar. A few times I found myself hugging a cliff face so that I wasn't bowled over by one.

I loved every moment of the day, even though I was suffering from flu-like symptoms. I was the only woman to carry my day bag. We arrived at base camp and the scenery was dramatic and beautiful – beyond words. We stopped and had our photos taken before getting some much-needed rest. I was beginning to feel some of the effects of being up so high. It was a big achievement for me.

That night in Gorak Shep the low oxygen levels got to me, and I also had a cold.

At Everest Base Camp welcome shrine

Everest Base Camp

Shrine to deceased climbers. This image also appears in the Introduction.

Daytrip to Kala Patthar and Trek to Pheriche – Wow and more wow!

The following morning, some of the group left at 3.00 a.m. to climb Kala Patthar and watch the sunrise. By this stage, many of the group were exhausted and after three nights of terrible sleep, I was in no state to go. Later, while trekking in Manaslu, I heard that sunset is a good time to go to Kala Patthar, and the photos taken then looked just as good. I think it was unwise of the touring company to have had this in the itinerary at that point. Instead, they could have given us a break. Later that day we trekked to Pheriche and spent the night there.

Pheriche

Pheriche to Khumjung – Memorials and prayer wheels

Khumjung is known for a school that was started by Sir Edmund Hillary in 1961. Since then, Sir Ed's Himalayan Trust has supported over sixty schools in the area. It was interesting to see how the locals still revere him. The weather closed in for our descent and it began to snow. It was amazing. What a beautiful valley to travel through with yet more mountains to view.

We stayed the night with the cousin of one of the Sherpa guides. The district is known for growing potatoes and everywhere cow dung was being used as manure in the fields. The people were busy ploughing and planting the potatoes from the year before. The potatoes were stored by burying them. That night I had potato instead of *chapatti* (wheat bread), which made for a nice change! I was also surprised by the use of yak poo on the burner, which was the first time I'd seen yak poo keep a fire awake! That night there was dancing. One of the Sherpa guides, Pemba, loved to dance – especially after a few drinks of the local drink, rice wine.

Khumjung to Monjo – Potato pancakes a local specialty

Six of us of from the group of twenty went for an overnight trek from Khumjung in order to see a particularly impressive view. There were two brothers in the group of six, one a lawyer and the other was in the army. One of the brothers just couldn't breathe and began crying. He had a serious case of altitude sickness. I approached Robin, the Australian nurse, and asked her to speak to him. She talked to him, rubbed his head and gave him Diamox, after which he was fine.

The views from Khumjung to Mt Everest were constant, it was right there, a majestic beauty surrounded by tranquil ranges.

We stayed the following night in a teahouse in the small village called Monjo. That night a little girl danced with flowing hands in sync with her entire body, with steps that matched the music.

The accommodation was adequate. Most of the time the accommodation was warm and comfortable and had wooden beds. The Sherpas slept on printed cushion covers, but they never complained. They always said they were comfortable.

Khumjung

Khumjung Secondary School, and Sherpa kids. Everywhere, most of these children seemed happy.

Khumjung

In front of the Edmund Hillary statue at Khumjung

Monjo to Lukla and return to Kathmandu

Monjo was roughly where Sagarmāthā National Park ended and the ordinary countryside began. But we didn't finish our trek till we got to Lukla, the airstrip town from which we had set out on the trail so many days before.

After we stumbled back into Lukla, we were each asked to give a $100 tip to the porters. Some members of the group felt $100 was a lot to give out as a tip. But as the porters only earned about $3 a day otherwise, it was clear that they deserved more.

I didn't have an issue with the tipping, as I had been informed beforehand that this would be expected at the end. It did amaze me that after the privilege of going to Base Camp, people could still think that way. The Sherpas had given us a monumental experience and got us all back safely.

Among us, there was a retired Kiwi couple. The husband had decided to collect interesting rocks along the way. He'd filled his pack with these rocks and one of the porters, who had to carry the bag in question, had removed the rocks. This porter was accused of stealing, and so wasn't going to receive any tip. I can understand that the man didn't want the rocks he'd collected removed, but everyone's bag had to be under a certain weight.

The same porter had helped an elderly Australian woman carry her day bag, even though he didn't have to. So, she decided that she would give him a $50 tip for the assistance. This meant he ended up getting half the tip he would otherwise have received (which was better than nothing).

After Lukla it was back to Kathmandu, the capital of three million with no traffic lights! We were soon to discover an area of Kathmandu that sold all Western-style food and where no hawkers were allowed. This was on the privately-owned Mandala Street in the Thamel district, which had great restaurants.

Mandala Street was a pedestrian-only street with pedestrian alleys off it. We ate lemon cheesecake with unsweetened yogurt in the Himalayan Java Coffee café, one of many in the area now, but also one of the most long-established. It was founded in 1999. I think teahouses were probably more the thing in the hippie era, when Kathmandu first became a popular destination for travelers and tourists.

Thamel and Mandala Street added up to a nice place to have some time out. They sold great coffee and desserts there; I went back a few times.

I stayed at the wonderful Kathmandu Eco Hotel, and I got to know all the staff there very well too. I met a guy called Bhimal, who wanted to explore the western part of Nepal, and meanwhile promoted honey made in caves by the Himalayan Giant Honeybee (*apis dorsata laboriosa*), which is over 3 cm, or more than an inch, long. Apparently the giant honeybees sip nectar from a poisonous plant that, in combination with other sources of nectar, gives the honey psychedelic properties. So that's a bit of something extra with your morning toast, I guess.

I was glad to have had such a good introduction to Nepal. It felt safe to have a guide and be taken up to Base Camp. A lot safer than I had expected. I also liked the fact that the company knew the area and the accommodation in the teahouses was a great experience. I created lifelong memories here and I am forever grateful.

Website version of this chapter

a-maverick.com/blog/everest-base-camp

References and Further Information

Anatoli Boukreev and G. Weston DeWalt, *The Climb: Tragic Ambitions on Everest*, N.Y., St Martin's Press, 1997

Jon Krakauer, *Into Thin Air: A Personal Account of the Everest Disaster*, London, Pan Books, 2011 (originally 1997).

For an account of the beasts of burden used on the trail to Everest Base Camp, see Alton C. Byers, 'Too many mules on the Everest trail', *Nepali Times,* 31 October 2019, on **nepalitimes.com/banner/too-many-mules-on-the-everest-trail/**. It seems that mules are a comparatively recent introduction, brought in to cope with increasing volumes of climber and trekker traffic, and that things were generally less pressured in the days when only yaks and dzos were used to carry goods in this area.

CHAPTER FIVE

Manaslu and Annapurna

So many other Everests around every corner!

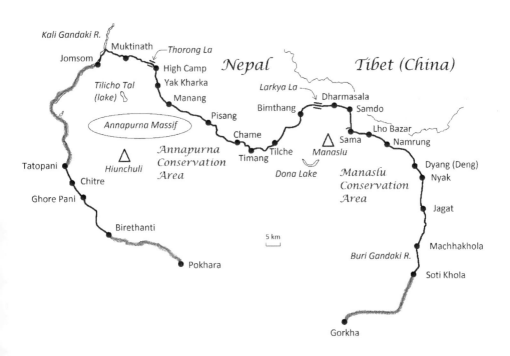

Map of the trek around Manaslu and Annapurna

AFTER Everest, I headed for the area of Manaslu and Annapurna, west of Kathmandu. My itinerary was hectic. It would take me from Gorkha to Namrung, Sama to Dharmasala, then the Larkya La (Larke Pass: La means pass in Tibetan and Sherpa), Bimthang and on to Pisang and the Lower Mustang district. After that would tackle the Thorong La Pass and finished up with Ghorepani, Annapurna and Poon Hill, in a locality known as Ghore Pani, or Ghorepani.

It was to be twenty-five days of straight trekking, including two very high passes in the form of the Larkya La or Larke Pass at 5,160 metres and the even higher Thorong La at 5,416 metres – an adventure like one I had never had before. It is an adventure that many people take on without any training, which is unwise in view of those hefty altitudes, nearly 17,000 feet at the Larkya La and 17,769 feet at the Thorong La.

To put things in perspective, the air pressure at these passes is barely over half what it would be at sea level. Apart from that, it also goes without saying that the environment is alpine, with some risk of avalanches.

And it also says something about the Himalayas that these are *passes,* between the actual mountains nearby!

In spite of what I've just said about Karma's Sunwise Mills, this hike is normally done anticlockwise. This is because the terrain slowly gets higher in the anticlockwise direction, whereas anyone who does it clockwise has to climb straight out of Jomsom, which lies in the deep gorge of the Kali Gandaki River, and go over the highest point, the Thorong La, straight away.

Everything's bigger in the Himalayas, and the Kali Gandaki Gorge is no exception: it is one and a half times as deep as America's Grand Canyon. That's why climbing up from Jomsom, clockwise, would be such a bad idea. You would have to go up the walls of the gorge by a vertical kilometer from Jomsom, which is itself at a textbook height for the onset of altitude sickness (2,743 m), to get to Muktinath; and more than a vertical mile after Muktinath to get to the Thorong La. Such a gut-busting ascent would make altitude sickness a near certainty, unless you were a fully acclimatized mountaineer who had been high up in the Himalayas for a while. The rule of thumb is that even a fit person should not ascend to a higher altitude by more than 300 metres a day once above 2,500 metres, if they haven't spent time at the higher altitude very recently.

At Thorong La, where there is only half as much oxygen as at sea level; the risk of serious altitude sickness for anyone coming up too fast is very real. On the other hand, no-one ever got altitude sickness by going rapidly down the hill.

Interestingly enough, Muktinath is a site of pilgrimage to which the trekker is slowly peregrinating for most of the journey, even if it is anticlockwise. And the hot springs of Tatopani are better enjoyed after most of the trek has been done, rather than at its beginning.

I was told Pokhara was a lovely lakeside town. I was also told that there had been only four guest houses as late as 1994. But by the time I visited, there were countless places to stay, including campsites that only cost one dollar a night.

Pokhara is sometimes referred to as Nepal's Phuket. Although it wasn't completely pristine and unspoilt, it was a handy base for place for a tourist or a traveller. I was able to get good food, a good hotel, and plan my upcoming adventure. I went searching, straight away, for a travel agency that could give me what I wanted: more than three weeks of hard trekking.

Day 1: **Gorkha to Soti Khola** (700 m) via bus - 5 hours

Day 2: **Soti Khola to Machhakhola** (869 m) - 6 hours

Day 3: **Machhakhola to Jagat** (1,340 m) - 6.5 hours

Day 4: **Jagat to Dyang** (1,860 m) - 6 hours

Day 5: **Dyang to Namrung** (2,630 m) - 6.5 hours

Day 6: **Namrung to Sama** (3,520 m) - 6 hours

Day 7: **Acclimatisation** (Monastery and lake sightseeing)

Day 8: **Sama to Samdo** (3,875 m) - 3.5 hours

Day 9: **Samdo to Dharmasala** (4,460 m) - 4 hours

Day 10: **Dharmasala to Larke Pass** (5,160 m)**, Bhimthang** (3,590 m) - 7 hours

Day 11: **Bhimthang to Tilche** (2,300 m) - 5.5 hours

Day 12: **Tilche to Timang** (2,750 m) - 6 hours

Day 13: **Timang to Chame** (2,670 m) - 4 hours

Day 14: **Chame to Pisang** (3,200 m) - 6 hours

Day 15: **Pisang to Manang** (3,540 m) - 6 hours

Day 16: **Manang to Yak Kharka** (4,050 m) - 5.5 hours

Day 17: **Yak Kharka to High Camp** (4,833 m) - 6 hours

Day 18: **Thorong Pass** (5,416 m) **and descent to Muktinath** (3,760 m)

Day 19: **Muktinath to Lubra-von Gompa** (Jomsom, 2,700 m) - 6 hours

Day 20: **Jomsom to Tatopani** (3,135 m) via bus - 4 hours

Day 21: **Tatopani to Chitre** (2,130 m) - 6 hours

Day 22: **Chitre to Ghorepani** (Poon Hill, 2,874 m) - 3 hours

Day 23: **Ghorepani to Birethanti** (1,039 m) **to Pokhara** (1,740 m) - 7 hours

Itinerary for Manaslu and Annapurna

Pokhara

I quickly found what I wanted. Tasi from Upper Mustang Treks and Expeditions was from the remote Mustang region himself, and I instantly trusted him. As compared to somebody from one of the agencies in Kathmandu where they had sales reps, Tasi seemed trustworthy and had an instant vibe of genuineness. He ran his own buses, so was an independent operator and I preferred that.

Mustang is a former mountain kingdom on the Tibetan border in the Annapurna region, mainly inhabited by Tibetans, though long independent of Tibet. Founded in the 1380s, and known historically as the Kingdom of Lo, Mustang collected customs duties from travellers between India and Tibet.

The historic capital of the Kingdom of Lo was Lo Manthang: a walled city north of Annapurna which remains pretty much the same as it was in the 1400s, its walls intact, today. We did not visit Lo Manthang as it is off the trekking path, but I would like to do so one day.

Mustang was taken over by Nepal around 1800 but retained its own monarchy: an arrangement known as suzerainty. In 2008, the last king of Mustang lost his job under the same reforms by which the Nepali monarchy was abolished.

When Tibet reverted to Chinese control in the 1950s, Mustang was cut off from the north and became isolated, with the result that Mustang became the last hold-out of really old-fashioned Tibetan culture. Upper Mustang remains the most strictly Tibetan part today.

(The name Mustang has nothing to do with the wild horses known as mustangs, which are from America. Yaks are more the thing in Mustang, Nepal.)

With Upper Mustang Treks I would be exploring the Manaslu Restricted Area, Larkya La, Annapurna and Thorong La. The Manaslu Restricted Area is one of the no-lone-zones I mentioned earlier, where you need a group of at least two and a guide. People say that Manaslu is restricted because you are only a few kilometres from the Tibetan (or Chinese) border for a good part of the trek.

After discussing the trip with Tasi, I met my guide for this part of Nepal, a man named Sampo, who was Tasi's cousin. I paid Tasi $750 and was given our itinerary and a permit for the Manaslu Restricted Area.

A mixed picture of words comes to my mind when I attempt to describe the next twenty-five days: poverty, happiness, hard work, beautiful mountains, good trekking, different food, no veggies, meat, oily fried food, sustainability amidst the poverty, solar, water tanks, and village hydro stations. I had not been to a Third World country in years before this trip to Nepal, but as a single woman with a guide I definitely felt safe. Being out of my comfort zone was not even a question.

On the first day of the adventure, we travelled by a rickety bus to Gorkha. From Gorkha we caught another bus to Soti Khola, driving through three districts in one day. It was 32 degrees Celsius – a really hot day for non-air-conditioned bus rides!

After the first bus, we caught a taxi and then had a real Nepalese experience on the second bus. It was called *The Titanic*. On this bus there were two people sitting on plastic barrels of petrol. Other cargo included sacks of rice, cement and goats. We travelled on the bus for three hours, with many people getting on and off. These people from the remote region of Manaslu were poor; it is a region that has only recently become a tourist destination. I saw dirt floors and canopy roofs on the houses. We crossed over bridges and drove along riverbanks. I was impatient for the mountains, but I knew it was a five-hour journey. Deforestation and the constant haze rising from the burning fields and the wood fires which the locals used for cooking meant there would be poor visibility until we got to the mountains where there were fewer people.

Sampo was educated at the Pokhara Tibetan Refugee School, and he spoke and read Tibetan. I was very fortunate, as he understood the language which was written on the Stupas and the prayer wheels which were present on entering and leaving every village.

Like Tasi, Sampo was from Mustang.

It was generally expected that when you hired a guide, you became responsible for them, and you had to look after them too. It was a terrible state of affairs, because they couldn't even afford to purchase equipment for themselves to do the treks properly – they worked hard for such little pay.

That night we stayed at one of the many new guest houses that were springing up in every town. These are not always owned by local people, which is a shame. The guest house was on the river at Soti Khola, at 700 metres elevation. The second night we stayed in Machhakhola, a town which had only one tap with running water for the whole town. I sat beside the tap for a while and the water was always running and always being used – for drinking, the brushing of teeth, and taken in buckets for the kitchen.

When I was there, Machhakhola was a Communist-ruled town, with red flags flying everywhere. According to Sampo, a lot of people had voted for a Communist party five years before, then after one year there had been a leadership change, but no change on the ground. The problem in Nepal was, apparently, that half of the political groups supported the Chinese government and the other half, the Indian government. Both parties were constantly debating Nepal's constitution and its borders, and nothing ever got done. Corruption was everywhere, with frequent power cuts and no industry or infrastructure development. As I've mentioned, most companies in the area tended to run from one a.m. to seven a.m. because that is when there were fewer people using the power supply.

I found that some of the younger generations in Nepal were finding it hard to get careers. Even educated people would struggle to earn more than $5,000 a year. Many have a child or two and often have to leave the country to make a living. Tourism is an answer to some of these problems. Outside of the tourism industry, the average wage is $80 per month.

In Machhakhola, I became acquainted with the people who would be my travelling companions over the next few weeks along with Sampo and the other guides; for we were now being combined into a larger group for safety's sake. I met an Irish couple called Mary and John, and two Israeli guys, Daniel and Jacob. These two were in their twenties and had no previous trekking experience. They just did it anyway. The next morning, we all left around the same time – 6.30 a.m., as by eleven a.m.

the heat was sweltering. Most days were to consist of six hours of trekking along trails and over bridges that spanned assorted chasms along the way. Fortunately, though one of the bridges we crossed was horrendous, most had been rebuilt.

Machhakhola to Jagat was only a 500-metre gradual climb, but really hot. The track was rugged and undeveloped, and you needed good trekking boots that went higher than the ankles, as it was so easy to trip and sprain them. We walked along rocky riverbanks and climbed up quaint, sculptured ladders. Basically, you had to be prepared for anything. Jagat was the official entry point to the restricted area, with a police post to pass through. In Jagat, we stayed at a lovely place just out of town between two high valleys. The guides had a light-hearted conversation about which Manaslu routes they had climbed. Sampo had great English and always told me what was being said.

We left Jagat and travelled on to Nyak. The Irish thought we had a 700-metre climb, but there were two Nyaks, one high and one low! That night we stayed in Dyang, the next village along, also known as Deng and listed under that name on Google Maps. If you did not stay at the Hotel Sangrila in Dyang (or Deng), then you could not stay anywhere apart from in your own tent, as the Sangrila was the only accommodation available. The village of Dyang barely existed, and the remarkable thing was that there was a hotel there at all.

Machhikhola

Bus 'The Titanic', and my guide Sampo under a precarious-looking gateway
near Namrung

At Dyang, a large French group of fifteen or so turned up as well. Some were quite unfit and already exhausted, even though they did not have to carry their own packs. I met a woman named Aldona who was part of this group. She was a French singer. I thought she was more of a French screamer after I heard her sing!

Sampo only got paid 1,200 Nepali rupees per day and his cousin, who actually owned the business, only got 1,000 rupees per day. This is from the 2,200 rupees per day I paid Tasi and is quite the norm. A Nepali rupee is officially worth just under one US cent, though of course it buys more locally. I won't bother making conversions in this book unless it's for emphasis, as you can just divide by a hundred to get a rough US dollar conversion, or by ninety to get a more accurate one.

Guides can eat for free in some of the teahouses and accommodations of the Himalayas after travellers are served, which can sometimes be as late as ten p.m. But in the Annapurna region, guides were charged 200 rupees per night at the teahouses, so the guides there rely all the more on tips.

Many of the guides have worked as chefs in top hotels in Europe and cook for their clients in order to make their meals more pleasant. When Mary's guide was around, our food was tastier. Sampo started cooking for me, beginning with French fries – a start! Dal bhat is the staple food in Nepal. It consists of boiled rice, steamed veggies or meat at times and a lentil soup – a great meal for dinner! Fried food tended to aggravate the cough I had caught at Everest Base Camp, producing mucus and phlegm, so I was trying to stop all fried food, as well as eggs and cheese where possible.

The availability of other food such as large spring rolls, pizza or pasta varied from town to town. There was no English breakfast here, and I ate chapatti and an egg for breakfast on most days. There was also *momo*, either fried or steamed (they are similar to Chinese dumplings), as well as tuna. When I considered eating chicken, I started inspecting freezers before I ordered. In fact, this was the case for any food with meat in it. Eggs or omelettes with Tibetan bread or toast were great. The only problem was that fruit got scarcer the higher you went.

After leaving Dyang, we had lunch in Ghap, a small town with just a school and a small restaurant next to a historic monastery. We left our bags out on the edge of the path. I tried to put mine inside the café, but it was too big, so I put it outside again and kept an eye on it.

In Ghap, we saw a French woman cleaning a Nepali child's cut finger. We sat there – me, the two Israelis and the two Irish – and simply admired her. Other children came around, as did the mothers, and the child marvelled at all the attention. When the French woman had finished, she noticed that she had been robbed. All her money, amounting to 20,000 rupees, was gone as was her credit card. She was very distraught. I gave her $50 and before long, she had more money than she did when she had started; she went from tears of sorrow to being filled with joy.

Further along, in Namrung, we had reliable wi-fi at last. However, the power did not on come on until 5.00 p.m. Sampo had commented that all the monasteries in this area were empty and that all the monks had left for a better life in Kathmandu.

The area was very poor, and we both agreed the people needed help. In Namrung we encountered government people and witnessed their meeting with the townspeople where they were learning how to build proper toilets. Namrung, at 2,630 metres elevation, was a larger town where there was a lot of construction going on cope with the increase in tourism.

Then we stopped at the town of Lho Bazar. It was at Lho Bazar that I caught my first sight of the mountain named Manaslu, which is 8,163 metres high and the eighth-highest mountain in the world.

A friend of mine named Victor was climbing Manaslu at that moment. Manaslu has a reputation for being extra-dangerous even by the standards of high Himalayan peaks, because almost no part of Manaslu above its base camp is safe from avalanches. Dozens of climbers have perished in avalanches on Manaslu. So, I was hoping for Victor's safe return. Readers will be glad to know he did get back, though without having made it to the top.

We should have stayed in Lho Bazar, which was a beautiful town, but we went on to Sama, at 3,520 metres. This was six hours of very steep trekking, often travelling straight up via sculpted ladders. After this, there was 300 metres of relatively flat land which provided a view of Manaslu Camp One, a camp for those ascending to the peak of the mountain.

Just before Sama, we saw a field of marmots, a kind of large squirrel which reminded me of puppies. Mary had a cough and I told her to get antibiotics before it became any worse.

Crossing a stream on a log bridge

Passing a mule on a narrow path

Wooden Steps

Trail Scenes

Lho Bazar, with a glimpse of Manaslu

Manaslu

In the hotels I always used my own inner thermal liner and sleeping bag to sleep in. At Sama, Sampo and I argued over hotels, and I ended up picking my own two-storey hotel; a beautiful place compared to the prison he wanted me to stay in. The food at the hotel I had chosen was wonderful, but Sampo wanted me to stay at the same hotel as the others. I put my foot down and refused.

I could not believe how some people treated their guides; some clients were completely oblivious to whether their guide had eaten in the morning or not. The services provided by guides also differed dramatically. The Irish couple's guide did not take any packs whatsoever; whereas Sampo took my medical kit with him and, as we got higher, also took on a few heavier things. Some guides did not have the right gear for the snow, and one enterprising guide charged commission on the jeep rides he organised. Sampo would not do this, but after we had a discussion as to why he refused, he agreed he would start charging commission.

Sama was our home for two nights as we were acclimatising to the altitude. We went on a day trip and visited the beautiful Birendra Lake and the Nubri Pema Decho Ling Monastery, which is nestled in the rocks halfway between the Birendra Lake and Sama.

Our next destination was Samdo at 3,875 metres. This took only three hours and was all uphill. Samdo was one only day's trek from the Tibetan (Chinese) frontier at the Gya La or 'Large Pass'. The Gya La is open for three months of the year: May, June and July. During this time, it is nearly impossible to pass as it is also the wet season. One of the guides did say it was easy to sneak through to China, however. Locals also said that people used to come over from the Chinese side, but they do not do that any longer as they have enough food nowadays and are not so poor. The Nepalese are not allowed to buy from China.

Instead, the food must come up on mules from Nepali towns, which makes things very difficult. Samdo had its own hydro station, as did many small villages. Solar panels were also used everywhere.

Birendra Taal (Lake), at Sama

Chez Karsang, at Samdo. Note the abundant firewood!

Yak Hotel and Restaurant, Samdo

In Samdo, we stayed in a large, cold lodge. It was horrid – Sampo's choice, of course! The kerosene fire did not come on until five p.m. and so we were all shivering. Aldona and the French trekkers stayed in small lodges and ate in the kitchen by the fire where the locals were cooking, which seemed much nicer and friendlier. I met a Dutch couple there who managed an up-market lodge in Tanzania. They had climbed Kilimanjaro, the highest peak in Africa at 5,895 metres. We also discussed the illegal ivory trade.

I had homemade yak butter, which was very delicious and watched the pregnant mares and other horses gallop around the fields. It had snowed, and everything looked very beautiful. At this elevation, one of the Israeli guys, Daniel, got dizzy and was helicoptered out. He said he had lost a lot of weight and was breathless and could not move. I suggested Diamox, two lots of 250 mg per day, but he wisely took a helicopter out before it got any worse; he was taking no chances.

Later that day on the way to Dharmasala (which is at an elevation of 4,460 metres, and not to be confused with the Dalai Lama's abode of Dharamshala in northern India), I saw a Chinese girl being carried out. She was completely unconscious. She had left that morning from Dharmasala and climbed 300 metres towards Larke Pass, but then could not move anymore. One porter for the Americans also had to leave because of altitude sickness.

I was alert to altitude sickness, because my bedtime reading was *Into Thin Air!* Krakauer talks about the prevalence of altitude sickness and also the prevalence of its denial among visitors keen to bag a peak, and even among some Sherpas as a matter of pride. But anyone is susceptible to this illness, including experienced Sherpas who had not had it in 10 years of climbing Everest.

I had been warned about Dharmasala but had not realised how bad it was. I would be staying in a windy tent with four other beds. Sampo was on the floor with just a mattress in the guides' tent. There was a dining room with an attached kitchen, twelve rooms for sleeping and about eight tents. The operation could house ninety-nine people in total. Aldona and Ian (another member of the group) were in the tent next to mine, meaning I could hear everything (which was not that great). The dining room had a very muddy floor, and your feet were pretty much sitting in water underneath a flimsy wooden table that could seat about sixty people. This was in a stone building which had no insulation and boards where the windows used to be. It was closed when the food ran out which could be anytime, but was usually during the wet months of June, July and August.

It was amazing what they produced in that kitchen: chapatti, eggs and Tibetan bread with eggs or jam. It is basic, hearty food, badly needed by weary travellers with symptoms of altitude sickness. On the morning we were there they ran out of eggs and were closing the next day.

To be able to build the hotel, the owner had been required to build a dam for the town. Otherwise, they would not have let him build even this rather basic complex.

There was some other accommodation in the town. But those huts were very basic and booked out most of the time. When we were there, a group of Czechs had booked them out. However, despite the basic accommodation, the views from Dharmasala were amazing, with the ranges forming a beautiful backdrop to the town.

The next morning, we started at 4.30 a.m. in order to see the first light. It was not as cold as I had expected it to be, and I was glad I did not wear my thickest thermals – just my light ones. I needed everything else, however. I also carried my own bag, which was another challenge, but I would have it no other way.

Sampo tried to get me to go faster, but on my earlier trip to Everest Base Camp the Sherpa guides had taught me to go slow and steady. I knew that I find it very hard to breathe while trekking higher than 4,800 metres. It annoyed me that he tried to push me, and we argued, as we always did, but only on the top of passes. We mostly worked it out.

One issue was that we needed crampons for the trek. I had left mine in New Zealand but could have purchased some in Kathmandu. However, we were never told that we would need them, so, of course, I had not bought any. Some of the guides were going to recommend that in the future, their companies made sure to remind their clients about the need for crampons.

Apart from my group of six making the ascent to the Larke Pass, there were six Polish tourists, ten French, ten Czech, six Russians, four Americans, as well as all the porters and guides.

We got to the top of the pass at about eleven a.m. There were some icy tracks, rocks and soft snow with long drops into crevasses. Before the descent, we had our lunch, and sitting there I realised there are so many near-Everests in this country of countless high mountains and amazing glaciers.

The descent was to Bimthang at 3,590 metres, so there was a drop of 1,500 metres. It was a very steep, rocky and icy descent. I went slowly, saving my knees, and we got to Bimthang at four p.m. There we stayed in the Himalayan Cottage. It had yellow cabins and an exquisitely carved lounge. I ate French fries and canned pineapple, which felt like Nirvana, and I washed all my clothes which I had worn for four days.

From Bimthang, we had a great view of the back of Manaslu. I tried to buy meat there, but I could not get any. The local people only ate superannuated yak – and that was way too tough for me.

In Bimthang, I overheard a huge argument. A Czech doctor was criticising the French group for leaving a woman on the pass. This was at five p.m. However, I had passed her earlier and she was with a porter. The other people in her group were fitter than her, so they had gone on ahead. She made it down in the end and arrived in Bimthang at ten p.m.

Earlier on, Sampo had pointed out sandalwood trees to me. These plants grew as small shrubs back in Namrung but here, they were tall trees. The wood from these trees is highly fragrant and used to make incense. It is burnt in the mornings in Nepal, as an offering to the gods. So too is the wood of juniper trees, which is also very fragrant.

The additional descent to Tilche was beautiful, with pink, red, and white rhododendrons in bloom – just amazing!

The descent from Bimthang revealed many new guesthouses. There were beautiful fields, but major deforestation was underway to cope with all the new buildings. Tilche was a jumble of hasty tourist developments and most people I met were staying in Dharapani and then taking jeeps out to Besisahar (another town full of motels!) and getting a bus to Kathmandu. We stayed one kilometre before the town at the Gorkha Guesthouse, which had beautiful views.

Sampo told me about the rather stressed lessee of this abode. The locals owed her a lot of money – six guys each owing six months' rent. Furthermore, she taught the cultural dances for which the tourism operators who owned the hotel were paid, but she received no money. The Czechs who were also staying at the Gorkha Guesthouse had brought their own beer, and on top of this, their guide argued with the hotel manager, saying he would not stay at a hotel where he could not hire a jeep.

I felt very sorry for the poor woman. Her husband had found a job in construction, but she still paid 60,000 rupees a month in rent, and I only paid 400 rupees for the night. While I was there, I had a hot shower and did some more washing.

We were now heading on to the Annapurna Trail, which passes through Tilche at 2,300 m, then Timang, Chame at 2,670 m, Pisang at 3,200 m, Manang, and then up again to Yak Kharka at 4,050 m, and finally, the Thorong La (Thorong Pass) at 5,416 metres. After that we would descend to Muktinath, which is a sacred place for both Hindus and Buddhists and has been a holy place for 4,000 years. We would then trek through Jomsom, Tatopani and Gorepani – an area which was deforested and disappointing. You did not need a guide there, really.

At Pisang, we stayed at the Lower Pisang Eco Lodge. On the way, we passed through two monasteries which were being built. It was the off-season and I thought I was the only one staying at the lodge for the night. Then eighty women arrived, including a nun, who were going to help with the renovations. They all burnt juniper wood in the morning.

We visited Upper Pisang, which was beautiful. It was a change of 300 metres in altitude from Lower Pisang. There were many hotels, and we encountered a lovely monk who gave us lemon tea and didn't ask for money in return.

At Manang we had beautiful views of the mountains – of the Annapurna massif – as well as of gardens and garlic. It was a tourist town, really. It was in Manang that I saw six posters of missing men – tourists in their twenties. They had all gone missing in the last six months and their families were offering rewards. Here, I also met an Irish guy who worked for orphanages in Kathmandu, and we discussed the expansion of poverty, professional begging and NGOs.

Along the way there were views of Hiunchuli, which I wanted to climb.

Before Thorong La High Camp there is a small settlement known as Base Camp. I stopped for a cuppa and was charged 200 rupees! That's about $1.80, which sounds reasonable, but it is very expensive for a country where a cup of tea in a teahouse normally costs one-tenth of that price. Of course, there's not so much competition at this altitude, and the customers are mostly from wealthier countries than Nepal.

Just before the Thorong La — more solar cookers!

Thorong La High Camp, with guide Sampo

Thorong La High Camp

We then walked on to High Camp at 4,880 metres. I was climbing 800 metres in a day to get there, but the very high altitudes on the trail so far had prepared me for that. Otherwise, the Thorong La would be a killer, from either direction.

Bad weather is also a major risk here. In October 2014, there was a devastating snowstorm in the area that left 43 people dead from exposure and avalanches, while 518 people had to be rescued. It was one of Nepal's worst trekking disasters, with several local people and 21 foreign trekkers killed on the Annapurna circuit alone. Such a tragedy shows that you have to be prepared for anything.

The accommodation at High Camp was all booked out and I ended up sharing a room with a Chinese guy from New York who got his porters to pack his backpack in the morning. To be honest, I was not very comfortable having strange men in my room. The next morning, we left early and went up and over the Thorong La, and then down to Muktinath. It takes about three hours to get up to the top of the pass (another 600 metres) from High Camp. This means going up by twice the recommended 300 metres to an altitude you have not yet attained, whether you have put in a big day of climbing the day before or not. Also, high winds often pick up mid-morning even in the absence of a lethal blizzard. So, you are in the danger zone, and you can't linger. In fact, I remember hurrying through parts of the Thorong La, thinking that I was in an avalanche danger zone. That was in May 2014, five months before the October avalanches.

Having said that, rather incredibly, there is another tea shop right at the top, open for four months of the year. Imagine living at the top of the Thorong La; that must be very close to being the world's strangest address. The hardest part of this section of the trek is perhaps the knee-killing descent (1,800 metres) to Muktinath, which definitely requires climbing poles.

Although some occasional through-routes and military roads in the Himalayas are, apparently, up to four hundred metres higher, the Thorong La is said to be the highest mountain pass in regular use anywhere. It is an intrepid journey in itself!

Thorong La Summit

Myself, and Sampo, at the Thorong La Summit

Muktinath

At Muktinath, near the village of Ranipauwa, I visited the historic temple. The temple is 4,000 years old and is sacred to

Hindus. There is also a Buddhist temple next door. Here Sampo collected holy water for his family, and I encountered naked yogis, or baba, who were talking to westerners about the meaning of life. I was not meant to go into the temple, but I did have a quick look.

The following day we left Muktinath and Ranipauwa, travelling along a road that used to be a walking track. We descended the hill to the caves of Kagbeni, near the Kali Gandaki River where we saw ancient fossils. Sampo told me how his father used to take him there when he was ten to look for fossils embedded in rocks. People used to live in the caves, but deforestation in the area had meant there was no longer enough water to make them habitable. Statues of Buddha remained, however – a relic of the former inhabitants.

We hired a taxi for $150 from Jomsom to Tatopani, as I had had enough of trekking beside dusty roads and needed a break. There was no way of taking a local bus, as it would just not make it on those roads. Along the way we saw a truck that had overturned, and then the axle of our own taxi broke. Sampo had to cut the tie off his pack for the driver to tie up the wheel rack which was connected to the axle.

In Tatopani, I stayed in a beautiful hotel. It was divine, and I relaxed by the river and went to the hot pools where I was the only woman. I also had my first clear view of the great mountain that is simply known as Annapurna.

After Tatopani, I began the climb to Chitre via Shikha – an ascent from 1,200 to 2,800 metres. It was a nine-hour day, as it was hellishly hot.

In Chitre, I met volunteer workers working with a local association. In 1995, a Dutch philanthropist named Jan Laan decided to help start an association which was to build a health care centre, help a local school and sponsor children. With the support of the United Nations, the local people also established a community enterprise called the Ghandruk Pure Water Factory, which draws its water from a high mountain spring and filters it to make doubly sure that it is safe.

The factory mainly sells the water in bulk to trekker hotels for ten rupees a litre. One of the motivations for starting the business was to solve a waste- disposal and littering problem. The idea was that with a supply of spring-water that was guaranteed safe, trekkers, wary of what came out of local taps, would no longer feel forced to keep buying bottles of drinking water that they could not refill and therefore had to keep throwing away, once empty, as they went along.

Given that hardly anything is more ideal for the supply of pure drinking water than a mountain spring, dragging commercially bottled water up from the city must surely have seemed like an exercise in hauling coals to Newcastle, in any case!

After Chitre, we went on to Ghorepani. This is a small town that is dominated by about twenty hotels as well as numerous restaurants. It is a good spot for honeymooners. There were seventy other people gathered at the Poonhill sunrise lookout, or perhaps even more. All the trees were gone, but the people there were not poor. From there, it was a final day's trek back to Pokhara, where I had a few days rest before my flight home.

While I was resting in Pokhara, I met Sampo's wife and daughter in the suburb of Riverside. They lived with Sampo's parents and brother. Sampo's parents did not want him to have more children – no money. They wanted him to go abroad for a job. His elder sister's children were with his grandparents in Mustang. His sister and brother-in-law work in France.

I met this guy who was a director of an orphanage, and who said many Nepalese families could not afford to have more than one child because of things like the cost of education, so they give them away to dodgy orphanages that got them to beg on the streets and more sinister things. He worked for an organisation that tried to reunite these children with their families and provided financial support.

Website version of this chapter

a-maverick.com/blog/manaslu-and-annapurna

CHAPTER SIX

The Three Passes

My toughest trek, made tougher by thinking about angry Sherpas who are paid the least and die first on the mountains, in earthquake and avalanche.

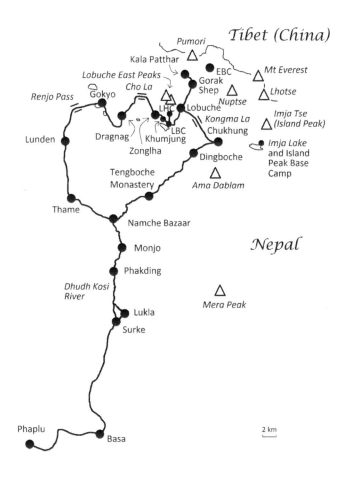

My Three Passes Route. This time around, I started from Phaplu, where there is also a local airport in addition to the one at Lukla, though in fact we drove to Phaplu from Kathmandu.

147

I WENT to Nepal for the second time in November 2015. My plan was to trek in the Khumjung region and climb Lobuche (6,120 m) and Island Peak (6,189 m). There had been a massive earthquake in April that had left almost 9,000 dead and hundreds of thousands homeless. I didn't witness the full effects of the earthquake, since I got there seven months after the quake. I did, however, see the beautiful statues, temples and historical sites that had been destroyed by the quake. Tourism had been badly hit. Friends back in New Zealand who had planned to go trekking in September and October had cancelled their visit and many tourists were doing the same.

Restoration of the Krishna Mandir, Patan Durbar Square. Photo by 'sushan116', 24 May 2017, via Wikimedia Commons, CC BY-SA 4.0.

What was just as noticeable at that time was the lack of fuel. Nepal had ratified a constitution in September after many years of political squabbling, but people in the southern plains were not happy with some of the provisions and they had sat down at the borders with India to protest. Nepal blamed India for siding with the protesters and imposing a trade embargo on the landlocked country, which relies on India for almost all its imports. India squarely denied any embargo and said it couldn't send in trucks if people were sitting on the bridge at the border and blocking land crossings. Whatever the case, it was chaos in the capital. People were lining up for fuel with their trucks and motorbikes. There were never-ending lines outside petrol stations but hardly any traffic on the road.

People were also worried they would have to spend the winter without any fuel for cooking and heating. Apparently, China was helping out by sending a large shipment of aviation fuel and petrol. The road from Lhasa to Kathmandu is a tough one; it's a dirt road in most parts and transportation is difficult. But people seemed optimistic about it. (The blockade would end, eventually, in early 2016, after several months, and after costing Nepal about $5 billion in economic damage, roughly the same as the dollar cost of the earthquake.)

I checked in to the Eco Hotel. The building was still standing, but it seemed like tourism had taken a double whammy with the earthquake and the fuel blockade. There were hardly any tourists. Western government travel warnings were making it harder for people to get insurance from their usual insurers.

I had pre-booked everything with a company in Kathmandu. It was going to be a 21-day trek and I would be climbing the two peaks I wanted to. The plan was ready, and I was looking forward to it.

The day after I arrived in Kathmandu, my trip was cancelled. I was quite horrified. I called up the company and told them I would never have come to Kathmandu if I had known the trip was going to be cancelled. They tried to book me for another trek and there was a lot of communication going back and forth. I didn't want to spend more time in Kathmandu than was necessary. For one, it's dusty. I'd much rather spend all that time walking along the mountains and climbing them.

The cancellation was understandable under the circumstances because fuel was in such short supply. If you couldn't work out a way of getting fuel, you couldn't transport tourists to the places they wanted to go to. But I had come from the other end of the planet and wasn't prepared for such a sudden change in plans. So, it was in the midst of desperation that I walked around town.

At the Eco Hotel, an Italian expedition had heard of my plight. I was introduced to the owner of the tour company. His name was Nuru Sherpa, and he sat down and drew an itinerary for me that covered 21 days. The plan was to drive to Phaplu, then trek to Namche Bazaar and then onwards through the Renjo Pass to Lobuche. We would then climb to the summit of Lobuche, return to the base camp, walk on through Kala Patthar and Chukhung to the Island Peak Base Camp, reach the summit and come back. I would return to Lukla and fly back to Kathmandu from there.

Day 1: **Arrive Kathmandu**
Day 2: **Phaplu to Nunthala**
Day 3: **Nunthala to Basa**
Day 4: **Basa to Surke**
Day 5: **Surke to Phakding**
Day 6: **Phakding to Namche bazaar** (3,400 m)
Day 7: **Namche rest day to acclimatise**
Day 8: **Namche Bazaar to Thame** (3,740 m)
Day 9: **Thame to Lunden** (4,380 m)
Day 10: **Lunden to Gokyo via Renjo Pass** (5,360 m)
Day 11: **Gokyo to Dragnag** (4,700 m)
Day 12: **Dragnag to Zonglha via Cho La Pass** (5,368 m)
Day 13: **Zonglha to High camp** (5,400 m)
Day 14: **High Camp to summit of Lobuche Peak** (6,120 m)
Day 15: **Lobuche to Kala Patthar** (5,545 m)
Day 16: **Lobuche to Chukhung** (4,730 m)
Day 17: **Chukhung to Island Peak base camp** (5,087 m)
Day 18: **Basecamp to Island Peak summit** (6,189 m)
Day 19: **Basecamp to Tengboche** (3,867 m)
Day 20: **Tengboche to Namche**
Day 21: **Namche to Lukla** (2,860 m)
Day 22: **Kathmandu**

Nuru's itinerary for the trek through the Three Passes

I frankly didn't want to be stuck in Kathmandu, so I decided to go with Nuru's plan. At the same time, the government had introduced a policy that required climbers to pay an insurance premium of $800 per Sherpa per peak, which I didn't mind paying. But it all meant my expenses shot up and I ended up paying a lot of money for the trip.

Nuru provided me with someone I will call my new guide, a Sherpa who was quite an angry man. The new guide came from Khumjung in the Khumbu region, and he had been to the

Tibetan side of Mt Everest. I had differences with him throughout the trip. He slept with a lot of cooks and cleaners from the hotels and put down my mountaineering skills, saying I did not know how to use crampons and so on. So, I did not trust him at all! My porter was called Mr Limbu and he was a lovely man. He was a Christian, which I thought was interesting because I hadn't met many Christians in that region.

We drove to Phaplu on the first day. The drive was interesting because there were almost no other vehicles on the road. We stayed at Phaplu that night and trekked to Nunthala the next day. From here on the type of hotel we stayed in became an issue. It started on day two and lasted throughout the trip. My new guide had been told by Nuru to save money and not to spend in excess of 1,500 rupees per customer per day. I refused to stay in cheap, dirty hotels. The last time I was in Nepal, I had paid around $1,300 for a 21-day tour. This time round I had paid close to $6,000. And for the type of money I had paid, there was absolutely no way I was going to stay in rat-infested places!

To add to that, I took ill on the second day. I don't know what I had eaten. I was puking. I had to be careful because I couldn't just eat anything. My new guide said that I wasn't up to it and that we wouldn't make it through the hard trip ahead of us. Those who have read my earlier books know that I have done my fair share of climbing and I am quite capable of using crampons, having used them on numerous occasions. But my new guide kept questioning my abilities and I was tired of it. I had bought my climbing gear in Namche Bazaar once we got there. I had hired boots from Nuru in Kathmandu, but only because I was travelling to several countries and boots were too heavy to take everywhere.

Nuru had also kept my passport. New Zealanders do not like their passports to be kept by tour organisers or agencies. I was nervous about it and attempted to get my passport back. I emailed the New Zealand representative in Nepal telling her that my travel agent had kept my passport. She was supportive and told me that she could arrange to have it sent to me, but I didn't want to risk having it transported simply because it could go missing and that would create a whole new set of problems. So, with all this, I was stressed enough and the last thing I needed was the additional stress of staying in horrible teahouses. I wasn't paying backpacker prices, so I didn't see why I should do the backpacker bullshit. In the end, I put my foot down and told my new guide we would stay where I wanted to stay and I would eat what I wanted to eat. It went on like that for the rest of the trip. We constantly bickered about the accommodation and food.

At the village of Basa, I stayed at Mr Limbu's house. I didn't really want to, but I did it out of politeness. I had said I would stay only where I could get hot water and I was starting to sound quite demanding. I ended up staying at his house all the same and I used the shower next door. The food was great! We ate freshly cooked chicken and I enjoyed it. I have always loved the food: dal bhat and the curries. And what I do like about Sherpa food is that it is not sweet. Mr Limbu's wife was a lovely woman. She cried and said she missed him, and that she didn't see why he had to be away all the time.

They had two sons. One was studying in Kathmandu, and the other had come home to take care of his mother. Mr Limbu's wife ran a boarding house for locals because some of them had no place to stay after the earthquake. At Basa, and in many places along the way, I was surprised at the number of Sherpas whose wives were running teahouses.

I was also quite surprised at the cost of education. Like Mr Limbu's son, my new guide's daughter was in a private school in Kathmandu. The fees were upwards of $120 a month, and so it was understandable to see people running multiple enterprises to meet these costs. My new guide had recently led a wealthy American up a peak (I think it was Lobuche). This man had a manufacturing company in the United States, and he had promised to get my new guide out of Nepal. So, unbeknown to his employer, my new guide was going to get a job in a manufacturing company and go climbing with this man in the States.

But at that time, my new guide was a very angry man. I didn't understand the anger many Sherpas felt until I watched the 2015 film *Sherpa*, which was made around the time of my first two trips to Nepal.

For instance, one of the issues described in the film *Sherpa* is the fact that while climbers and trekkers might only briefly or occasionally pass through a certain danger zone in the mountains, at risk of avalanche or ice-fall or slipping and falling oneself, Sherpa porters bringing up the supplies often have to go back and forth through these danger zones with the regularity of the delivery service they provide. Even the guides will, obviously, do the same route again and again.

There had been a fall of overhanging ice on Mount Everest in 2014, reported in the media as an avalanche, that killed sixteen Sherpa guides and porters. The route that passed through the spot where the ice fell was changed to try and minimize the risk of this type of incident, which had happened before, from happening again; though the risk probably cannot be eliminated entirely so long as people are in the mountains at that altitude.

Plus, while many of the clients are wealthy and pay a great deal to the guiding companies that lead them up the highest mountains, Sherpa porters earn a comparative pittance, in addition to bearing so many risks along with their burdens. According to *Sherpa*, Everest porters earned $5,000 in the two-month climbing season in the mid-2010s; which was far more per day than the porters on my treks but still not a heck of a lot. The whole Himalayan mountain business is in some ways the last vestige of a primitive, labour-intensive economy of the sort in which masses of toilers are paid next to nothing.

A porter at Basa

The Sherpas complained that the Nepalese government collected large amounts of money from foreign expeditions and their permits but did little for Sherpas either in terms of their conditions of life, or their safety, even though the whole mountaineering business rested on the Sherpa's back both literally and in a wider sense. There were acrimonious negotiations, boycotts and strikes aimed at getting the death compensation for mountaineering Sherpas, which had stood at only $4,000, increased to $20,000. This demand was accompanied by a range of others, including more help for the injured and disabled. The Sherpas made some gains in the short run, including a rise in the death compensation to $10,000. It's because of these improved benefits that my premium went up. You wonder what mountaineers and trekkers would have to pay if the Sherpas got a really good deal as opposed to merely not being exploited quite as badly as before.

The subsequent 2015 avalanche at Everest Base Camp, which was triggered by the earthquake and killed at least twenty-two, also claimed many Sherpas along with foreign climbers.

A number of foreign countries, including New Zealand, have their own nationals working as guides working in Nepal, and they are paid well – much better than the local Sherpas. When disasters strike, it's usually the latter that die. In *Sherpa*, some of the Sherpas guiding a French expedition refused to continue as guides on perilous climbs. They said they wanted to be fathers, see their children born and not simply risk their lives guiding people up Everest without adequate financial compensation. They went back to being farmers, which is what they essentially are when they are not working as guides. They grow fantastic food!

(Local mountaineering guides and porters are generally all referred to as Sherpas by the way, though many are not ethnically Sherpa.)

A lot of young people also resented the stereotype of the smiling Sherpa. Sherpas, including Tenzing Norgay, are always depicted as an ever-smiling race. There wasn't much to be smiling about; forget smiling all the time. Not under the present circumstances, at least. But I didn't understand this resentment at that time, and I certainly didn't understand why my new guide was angry. He kept putting me down and questioning my mountaineering skills. He seemed to have no intention of taking me to the summits and that really pissed me off! Of course, if I had slept with him, he probably would have taken me to the top of the mountain. I have had the same old rubbish in New Zealand as a single woman. If you are a guy, you wouldn't have to be gay and sleep with your guide to please him. What a load of crap!

The night at Basa was the night of Diwali. It is an important festival in Nepal as in other parts of South Asia. To me, it felt like another Christmas night in Queenstown with a lot of drunken men outside. As a single woman, I didn't feel safe going out or walking about on my own. We left Basa the next morning and set out for Namche Bazaar. We had night halts at Surke (2,290 m) and Phakding (2,610 m) on the way.

We reached Namche Bazaar (3,340 m) on the sixth day and stayed there for one more day to acclimatise. We then went to Thame and from Thame to Lunden. Many of the teahouses were already closed and we were lucky to find accommodation that night. In Lunden we met a Sherpa who worked in Japan as a cook during the winter months when it's not the climbing season. We stayed up late and talked about the yeti. I hadn't heard many tales of the yeti before, and it made for an interesting conversation.

In Lunden, and throughout my journey, I was struck by the resilience of the people. The earthquake had destroyed their houses and hurt the tourism industry, but the Sherpas were absolutely resilient. They picked themselves up and started repairing and rebuilding. Some of them had received international aid and others were waiting for compensation from the government, but they didn't sit back and wail about the earthquake and wait for help. They took their tools and started carving stone bricks and rebuilding their houses the traditional way. There was a lot of activity going on wherever I went, and it was uplifting.

The Sherpas were also missing the trade with Tibet. They used to have an active trade across the border, and they bought their clothes and a many other things from Tibet. Five years earlier, the Chinese government had closed the borders and that killed the trade. What a shame! In a few parts, however, people still trade with the Tibetans on certain days on the year.

The next day we had to cross the Renjo Pass to get to Gokyo. It wasn't easy! The Three Passes trek is the toughest of the three that I have described up to now. In my chapter on the Everest Base Camp trek, I told a story about a retired couple who came with us: the one where the old man was a bit of a rock-hound and would have added to his collection, if their porter hadn't quietly got rid of the rocks. Well, anyway, I don't think you would come across too many retired couples on the Renjo Pass.

The other thing, which makes it tougher still, is that there are fewer towns and villages along the way than on the Everest Base Camp or Annapurna/Manaslu treks. As such, you end up in a tent quite a bit, making your own tea.

Making our own tea in the tent

We started from Lunden at three in the morning with our torchlights and crossed the pass which is at 5,340 metres above sea level. We stayed the night at Gokyo (4,750 m) and what a beautiful place it was!

The Gokyo lakes, the highest lake system in the world, were beautiful; the environment was scenic and Gokyo Ri peak was in the background. It was quite the perfect place! I didn't really mix much with the locals there. My new guide, on the other hand, used to try and chat up every female cook that we came across.

With my guide and porter near the Gokyo Lakes

The main Gokyo lake with a communal building at right, for scale

The Gokyo Lakes and the village of Gokyo

The day after that, we went to Dragnag, which is at the same altitude and was just as lovely.

After Dragnag, we headed to Zonglha via Cho La – another pass, located at 5,420 metres above sea level – and that wasn't any easier. I found it quite difficult, but I have never really suffered from mountain sickness, as I tend to go slow and breathe a lot, and that helped me get across.

From Zonglha (4,830 m), we went to the High Camp at the base of Lobuche. Once again, I decided where we would spend the night because I was certainly not staying where my new guide wanted me to. We ended up staying at a new place that had been opened by a young guy. He had received some subsidies from the government and the place was worth staying at. But this young man was quite angry. He jokingly said he would go to India, pretend to be an Islamic terrorist and blow up something there. All this, of course, was about the fuel blockade that followed close on the heels of the devastating earthquake. I looked at him and I thought to myself that if this is what some Sherpas high up in the Himalayas think, then a lot of the bombs that are set off by so-called Islamic militants probably aren't about Islamic extremism at all!

We were to leave for Lobuche East Peak the next morning. The peak is 6,145 metres above sea level. I met an English couple who had been to the summit and back. They told me that if we left at three in the morning, reached the summit by eleven a.m. and then returned straight away, we would be fine. I had all my gear and was ready for the climb. But my new guide clearly had no intention whatsoever of taking me to the top. He didn't want to help me rope on to him – absolutely nothing! It was four a.m. by the time we even started, and he just walked on ahead. In the end, I decided I was not going to go with him; it just wasn't going to happen. I didn't need to be with someone I didn't trust. And though having paid all that money, I didn't trust him.

We didn't go to the summit. We went to Kala Patthar and came back to Lobuche. The next day, we went to Chukhung (4,730 m) and stayed there for two nights. We were to go to the Island Peak Base Camp from there, climb to the summit and return to Base Camp. But as I didn't trust my new guide, I didn't want to climb Island Peak, also known as Imja Tse, with him. I just sat in Chukhung looking at Ama Dablam instead.

Ama Dablam means Mother's Necklace. This really spectacular-looking mountain bears that name because the highest of its peaks seems like a mother cradling her children, while the hanging glacier resembles a necklace. It was a beautiful sight and I looked at it for three days and then grew tired of it. I became bored with it all. I was bored of being with a guide, I was bored of being with a porter, and frankly, I could well have done it all by myself!

While in Chukhung we stayed at a teahouse, and I got talking with the owner. He was a lovely guy and we talked for long into the evening about yeti folklore and snow leopards.

Ama Dablam

The yeti, also historically known as the abominable snowman, is the Himalayan version of 'bigfoot'. It is a hairy, ape-like humanoid that is supposed to live high up in the mountains of the Himalaya. He told me that the locals call it 'Meh-Teh', and that stories get passed down through the generations.

Snow leopards were also quite common around the more remote villages of the Himalayas. Like the kea of New Zealand, snow leopards were often seen by humans despite being quite rare, for both species were drawn to where people were in the hope of some kind of an easy feed. Obviously, this was more of a problem with leopards than with a cute green parrot.

The owner also told me about winter when the temperatures are far too cold and the weather is extreme, turning the beautiful mountains into harsh, white, frozen lands. The mail didn't even get delivered, and most locals departed to stay in warmer areas where they could find work. He himself left for Japan during the coldest six months of the year, to work as a chef. He also told me Tibetan traders used to frequent his village, but because of tensions with China, they had closed the borders and now they did not come. He said it was sad because he liked the company and news from other villages and Tibet that the traders would bring.

We went on to the Island Peak base camp and on to Tengboche. At 3,867 metres, Tengboche is at a much lower altitude. I had been to Tengboche on my earlier trip, and again, I decided where we stayed. I met a nurse there who told me she had established a medical centre in Langtang with Australian volunteers working there. The region that takes its name from the village is halfway between the Annapurna-Manaslu region and the Khumbu (Everest) region and considered the third major trekking region in Nepal. Langatang isn't as famous as Annapurna-Manaslu and Khumbu, mainly because it doesn't have such famous mountaineering destinations. But that may be neither here nor there if you are a trekker.

Tragically, 243 people were killed when a gigantic landslide buried the village of Langtang during the 2015 earthquake or a few moments afterward: mostly villagers, but also some dozens of trekkers. The nurse I was talking to, and her husband, were supposed to be there on the day of the earthquake. Thankfully, none of her staff had disappeared and they had re-established the village in tents for the time being. (Update: the village is being rebuilt, and it's said that the best way to help the people of Langtang is to go trekking there. It won't be as crowded as the more famous locations of Khumbu and Annapurna-Manaslu!)

From Tengboche, we went back to Namche Bazaar and then to Lukla. We took the flight from Lukla to Kathmandu and my 21-day trek came to an end. I had quite a few disappointing moments and thought there were many ways in which it could have gone better.

However, I had met two mountaineers who had wanted to climb Ama Dablam the year before, but when they got there, the weather was so bad that they couldn't do any trekking at all. And I remember what they told me: You could choose to leave Nepal with wonderful memories – take it for what it is and come back and do things again. Or you could choose to leave with nasty memories. I then decided I was going to leave Nepal with all the great memories.

If I were in a position to climb Mt Everest from Nepal, I still wouldn't want to do it. I think it's all become an industry and I don't like it. I really did notice a lot of anger during my journey as well. The Sherpa guides are angry, and the people are angry, though the situation is completely understandable. I would prefer to do it from the Tibetan side instead because there are fewer people doing that.

My guide told me that Sir Edmund Hillary was his hero, and that he was very grateful for all the things that Sir Ed, as we tend to call him in New Zealand, had done for the Sherpa people. He also said that you could go skiing at Khumjung during the Christmas period. I hadn't thought about Himalayan skiing in all this time! There are in fact several ski resorts in the Himalayas, with China currently proposing to build the highest, at up to 4,500 metres, in Tibet.

A bit later, I decided to go back to Nepal and climb Island Peak, which I hadn't managed to get up before, and Mount Mera. I'll describe whether I succeeded, or not, a little further on in Chapter 11. Meanwhile, my next stops were to be in India and Pakistan!

Website version of this chapter

a-maverick.com/blog/the-three-passes

CHAPTER SEVEN

Strategic Sikkim

Loved Gangtok Town, no other Westerners!

The strategic location of Sikkim. The state, contested in the past by both India and China, lies in close proximity to the narrow neck of Indian territory called the Siliguri Corridor, only 22 kilometres wide at its narrowest, which if interdicted would entirely cut off eight eastern states of India including Sikkim. The pointy bit of Tibet to the east of Sikkim is the Chumbi Valley, which some Indians have gone so far as to call "a dagger drawn at India's heart."

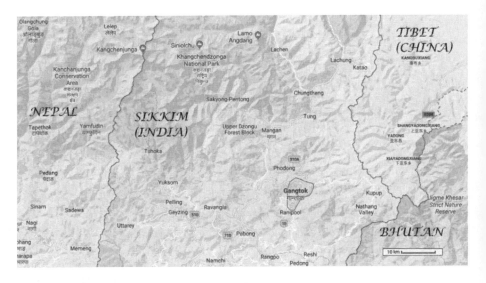

Four nations very close together: A closer view of central Sikkim and environs. Kangchenjunga, the third highest mountain in the world, is on Sikkim's border with Nepal, near the top of this map. Background map data ©2018 Google (country names overlaid).

I HAD always been interested in visiting Sikkim. It's a country influenced by Buddhism, and I was really fascinated by Buddhist culture, art and ideas. Sikkim is located between Nepal and Bhutan, and was a semi-independent monarchy until 1975, when it gave up its monarchy and became a state of India. But I was to find that getting to Sikkim brought its own set of challenges!

I planned to reach the state of Sikkim by train from the great Indian city of Kolkata, formerly Calcutta. My Namaste Tours guide took me to the station in Kolkata where I was to board the train to the New Jalpaiguri station in Sikkim. It was almost an eighteen-hour journey, and then on top of that I would have

170

to take a taxi from there to Gangtok, the capital of Sikkim, which meant an overnight stay on the train.

I remember going to catch my train at the Howrah Junction Station. Dust and a damp smell of rubbish greeted me as I entered the platform. I was amazed at the number of people who were lying on cardboard (if they were lucky) and others straight on the dirty, rubbish-littered floor around the station. There were children and elderly sleeping huddled against pillars and walls. It blew me away and is a memory that I will never forget.

Trains are a major mode of travel for people in India and my biggest fear was falling sick and not being able to complete my planned journey and treks. The last thing I wanted was to be shacked up in a cockroach-infested carriage on the train, vomiting my guts out. When the train rolled into the platform, I found out that I had a second-class ticket. There was no way I was going to travel second class in an Indian train; no offence, but that is just too rough for me.

I decided to abandon the trip and asked my guide to take me to a hotel. The guide kept asking me for money all the way to the hotel, which was annoying. I had already paid $1,500 to Namaste Tours in New Delhi to organise my trip, and I wasn't going to pay any more money. At one point, I had to firmly tell him that he should get his payment from the Namaste Tour agency in New Delhi, as I had already paid them, and I wasn't paying any more.

I stayed the night at a hotel in Kolkata near the airport and the next day got a flight to Bagdogra and then a taxi to

Gangtok. But my Sikkim adventure didn't end there. The drive from Bagdogra was through the mountains, and there was a checkpoint where foreigners had to register before entering the state. I encountered the same problem as I had had in New Delhi. I stopped, and the customs guard checked my passport and said I had no visa for India on my passport. I told him that I had a 'visa on arrival' and tried to explain what it meant and how it was different from the regular tourist visa.

But he didn't seem to know anything about visas-on-arrival. I was surprised that the visa policies were not communicated to customs officers in areas far away from New Delhi. I was detained at the checkpoint for over two hours, and I thought I would soon get arrested. Finally, my taxi driver came in and spoke to the customs guard and he let me go. Later, I found out that I could have taken a helicopter from the Bagdogra airport, albeit at extra cost and peril, and it would have saved me all this trouble.

I was relieved when I reached Gangtok and decided I was going to chill out for the next ten days. I found a room in the bottom floor of a hotel for $25 a night and a phone. There were nice restaurants. The only issue was that I rarely saw any Western tourists. Everyone looked at me as if I was a weird creature and after a while it felt like I was in a zoo. Whenever I saw a Westerner, we said hello and I would end up having dinner with them. It was quite hilarious.

Gangtok was a beautiful town with views of Kangchenjunga, the third-highest mountain in the world.

Gangtok tenements

Clouds rolling in over the city of Gangtok

No honking in the street the state governor inhabits!

Gangtok Markets

Gangtok's Aerial Ropeway. From Wikimedia Commons, by 'kalyan3', CC-BY-SA 2.0 (2007)

Kangchenjunga as seen from Gangtok at dawn. From Wikimedia Commons, by 'Stguin', CC BY-SA 4.0 (2015). The image has been corrected for brightness and contrast a little for this book, as the original is very soft.

Nepali (Nepalese) is the main language, but there is a strong Tibetan influence also. There were many shops selling mountaineering gear and I would have liked to do some trekking, but I would have needed a permit. They also told me that it was the end of the season and so I decided to enjoy myself. And surprise… surprise… I met a guy who was gay, and he said he had about five dates that night. It was through a dating app called Grindr. I thought, my goodness! I could have gone on the 'straight' equivalent of that, but I had no energy.

From Gangtok I visited Yuksom, the first capital of the ancient kingdom. Amazing. It was the Buddha's birthday, and I went to the local monastery and gave a donation. I also met an interesting guy called Claudio. He was Icelandic and had once lived in Germany. After his father passed on, he had received some inheritance and was living in different parts of the world. He had lived in South India for six months and the last time I saw his post on Facebook, he was living in Malaysia. I could find that an attractive option. We went trekking around Yuksom. And that was interesting, with tree ferns like those in New Zealand: a country that was connected to India in the dinosaur age, as improbable as that might seem now.

A tree fern similar to New Zealand Dicksonia *species (hairy tree ferns)*

We saw how the people were making rice flour decorations for the Buddha's birthday. The food was awesome. I also got caught up in a funeral procession in Sikkim. We were invited to eat, which I couldn't believe. It was really nice.

Corn sellers on the road in Sikkim

A drive in the country outside Gangtok.

Yuksom is also the basecamp for trekkers to Kangchenjunga. I met a guy whose father had climbed Mt Everest with Sir Edmund Hillary. He said that in around 1958-60, Nepalese people in this region were given a choice to live in Darjeeling, which is part of India, or in Nepal. Apparently, many Sherpas decided they wanted to live in India.

In 1962 there was also a war between India and China, which focused attention on the strategic location of Sikkim and contributed to its eventual incorporation into India. This was done lest the Chinese move into Sikkim from Tibet's adjacent Chumbi Valley, and then from Sikkim down through Darjeeling to block the Siliguri Corridor: a meandering corridor which connects the easternmost states of India, a region historically known as Assam, to the rest of India.

A large area of historical Assam used to be part of Tibet, before being carved off by the British in the 1800s. When India became independent in 1947, this area was not given back to Tibet.

As with Hong Kong, Macau, Taiwan and the rest of Tibet, China claimed that this part of Assam, too, was rightfully its own territory.

It was in Kashmir, where some parts of the territory were also viewed by the Chinese as rightfully part of China's Xinjiang Province, and in Assam, that the war of 1962 was fought. The war ended after a month, when the Chinese rather unexpectedly declared a ceasefire, and a withdrawal in Assam. Though China largely got what it wanted in the west, its rulers may have feared the eventual arrival of Indian reinforcements via the Siliguri corridor in the east.

As if toppling three dominoes in a row, by gaining control of Sikkim first, then the Siliguri Corridor, and then Assam, China might have been more successful in the east. Indeed, a more victorious China might even have been in a position to drop a fourth domino by moving its troops south and west toward to the Bay of Bengal, with only a little bit of Bangladesh in the way at the very end.

Since the late 1940s, when both countries had become independent from Britain, Sikkim had been an Indian protectorate, an 'associated state' as it was called. All the same, Sikkim was still independent of India in other ways, and thus capable of forming a government friendly to China. By the mid-1970s, the rulers of India had come to the view that it was best to fully incorporate Sikkim into their own country as a new state, the better to remove any temptation on China's part to flick over the first domino on any renewed road to the conquest of Assam. The annexation was done by way of a 1975 referendum, in which a majority of the votes cast in Sikkim endorsed the idea of full union with India.

The mountaineer's son also told me about Darjeeling's famous mountaineering school, the Himalayan Mountaineering Institute, where the statue of Tenzing Norgay shown in the introduction to this book stands. Though part of another state of India today, Darjeeling also used to be part of the territory of Sikkim.

To sum up, I really enjoyed Sikkim—it's a special place. And probably still off the beaten track for Western tourists, as well!

Website version of this chapter

a-maverick.com/blog/strategic-sikkim

Note: The modern Indian state of Assam is one of seven states to the east of Darjeeling, Siliguri and Bangladesh. Historically, though, the name Assam referred to all of India east of those parts, and that is the sense in which I have used the word, above.

CHAPTER EIGHT

Chitral and the Hindu Kush

Snowfall, avalanches, a threatened tribe and people who speak four languages

Map of Northern Pakistan, Kashmir and the Hindu Kush which runs between Kashmir and Afghanistan

Map of the Chitral (properly, Chitrāl) Region, with addition of country names and location of the Lowari Tunnel and Zondrangram Valley. Background map data ©2018 Google

THE majestic Hindu Kush mountain range is every mountaineer's dream. In the east, it is part of the Pamir range where the borders of China, Pakistan-controlled Kashmir and Afghanistan meet. In the southwest, the mountains run through Pakistan and Afghanistan, merging with other mountain ranges in Iran. The highest peak is the 7,708-metre Tirich Mir near the Pakistan-Afghanistan border. Tirich Mir overlooks the town of Chitral – which is pronounced with a long a, and thus also spelt Chitrāl – and sticks out from its surroundings by nearly four thousand metres. As a local landmark, Tirich Mir is hard to miss.

K2, the second-highest mountain in the world is also located near here in the Karakoram Range.

The region is stunningly beautiful but has suffered from the war in neighbouring Afghanistan and the sectarian violence in Pakistan. The Pakistani Taliban took control of the Swat Valley east of Chitral between 2007 and 2009, but apart from the Swat Valley, the region was considered a safe haven for trekkers until June 2013, when militants shot dead ten mountaineers at the Nanga Parbat base camp in Gilgit-Baltistan, an area east of the Swat Valley. Ever since, most countries have issued strict travel warnings for Pakistan. The country has itself become something of a police state, with many travel checks for its local inhabitants.

(I have a reference to a media story about the Nanga Parbat attack at the end of the present chapter, plus references to several other things as well.)

The Pakistani Taliban are the cousins of the religious extremists who took over Afghanistan in the late 1990s and harboured Osama Bin Laden, mastermind of the 9/11 attacks, who was eventually tracked down and killed by the Americans at Abottabad in Pakistan in 2011. Bin Laden's safe house was located less than a mile from the Pakistan Military Academy, and it has been suggested that this almost ridiculous degree of proximity implied a degree of protection from elements in the

Pakistan security Establishment, which had been unable to track him down. Certainly, it is true that the Pakistani Taliban have many sympathisers in sections of Pakistani society. And the Afghan border regions, historically known as the North-West Frontier, have been a Taliban stronghold, as they were of various fierce warrior societies and sects in the past. For instance, the legendary Khyber Pass, the subject of many a poem by people like Rudyard Kipling, is on the border of today's Pakistan and Afghanistan. In Auckland, New Zealand, we have roads with names like Gilgit Road and Khyber Pass Road, a link with the days when Victorian armies were posted to what was then the North-West frontier of British India.

By staying fairly close to Chitral town and the peaks to its north, we were headed for what was supposedly still a fairly safe part of the local frontier-lands, an area that was very popular with Pakistani holidaymakers themselves.

(Having said that, it's the foreigners who stick out the most. At the time of writing, the New Zealand travel advisory for the region featured a red triangle with an exclamation mark in it and the advice **Do not travel**, in bold letters, to anywhere that I'm going to talk about in this chapter, including Chitral. The rest of Pakistan merited an orange triangle with an exclamation mark in it. The Australian advisory was similar but classed the urban areas of Chitral and Gilgit and their environs as orange, though anywhere near the Afghan border was still red. Such is the situation. Chitral town itself has suffered a string of bomb attacks over the years, including some in 2018.) Travel insurance is something you need to re-check in dangerous regions, by the way. If your embassy says not to go there or to proceed with caution, there is a good chance your normal insurance cover won't apply either.

I arrived a year after the Nanga Parbat attack. I was part of a team with Patricia Deavoll and Chris Todd, New Zealand's best-known mountaineers. Pat was familiar with the region, as they had been there before. This time they were going to climb the Roshgol Glacier in the Hindu Kush from Chitral, and then attempt either of two unclimbed southern faces – the southeast face of Shakhawr (7,116 m) or the south face of Languta-e Barfi (6,827 m) – or both. Few expeditions have been up to the Roshgol, and none had previously reached the head of the glacier. This expedition was sponsored by several organisations, including Earth Sea Sky, Southern Approach, W. L. Gore, Back Country Cuisine and the New Zealand Alpine Club.

I first heard about the trek from Pat's Facebook post. She was looking for people to accompany her and I thought, why not. Because of the conflict in Afghanistan, the local theatre of the so-called War on Terror, I felt it was important for me to visit Pakistan and see what this country was like for myself. There was so much hardship and poverty in that beautiful country already. Additionally, the spillover of conflict from Aghanistan had had a devastating impact, not only in the physical sense (with drone attacks), but also psychologically. I emailed Pat, and there it was – all done.

The trek was organised by Terichmir Travel, a trekking agency owned by the late Abdur Razaq, who was to perish in a flood in 2017. Abdur himself was to be our guide.

A family business based in the town of Chitral, Terichmir Travel has survived the loss of Abdur and remains in operation, at terichmirtravel.com. It is currently managed by Abdur's nephew, Hussein Ahmed. The firm is named after Tirich Mir, the local landmark whose name can be spelt in various different ways. Even pre-Covid, I was that sure all those negative travel advisories couldn't have been helping Abdur's firm.

I was supposed to meet up with my climbing partner, David, but what with one thing and another, I wasn't able to for a while. We finally caught up at Dubai airport and shared the same flight to Islamabad. I was mostly travelling on my New Zealand passport, but had applied for a visa to enter Pakistan on my UK passport. Razaq was anxious about this and thought my UK passport may land us in trouble. He said the UK was perceived as an aggressor nation, unlike New Zealand, and so we were to be prepared for surprises.

As I was in Pakistan, I thought I would be required to wear a head scarf in accordance with conservative Muslim traditions, yet no such request was ever made of me. I still wore my scarf, but many people thought I looked like a bride. I was wearing the churidar-kurta I had bought in India – the *kurta* was a knee-length top with elbow-length sleeves and the *churidar* was a fitting pair of trousers with the kurta over the top. There was an issue with this outfit, but it wasn't the headscarf. It was the bare forearms, common enough in India but apparently too revealing by Pakistani standards. In the end, I bought a jacket with longer sleeves and a dress in Chitral.

From Chitral, we had a six-hour drive to Zondrangram. It's a beautiful place at the junction of the Tirich and Roshgol rivers, close to the Afghan border. We received a rapt welcome upon arrival in Zondrangram and stayed two nights at the home of Professor Rehmat Karam Baig, an expert on the cultures of Chitral, who also operate the tour guiding firm Hindu Kush Adventure Guides. Professor Baig has written several books on the Hindu Kush, and even one on the misrepresentation of Islam by extremists.

Zondrangram

We talked about Pakistan, and I learnt that Pakistan is a mostly Sunni Muslim country with a Shi'a Muslim minority.

The Sunni and Shi'a are the two main branches of Islam. In Islam, there are also the Isma'ili, followers of a historical imam named Isma'il, who are frequently thought of as a third branch though they are actually an offshoot of the Shia; and Sufi, who are not so much an actual theological branch as rather the practitioners of a mystical form of worship that involves trances and meditation. The name Sufi comes from the Arabic word for wool, a common garment of hermits. There are also many other religious and ethnic minorities in Pakistan, including the Kalash, whom I was soon to meet in Chitral.

When the Taliban went through Chitral, girls couldn't go to school. But all the women in Professor Baig's family were university-educated and spoke three languages in addition to the Pakistani official language of Urdu; which is much the same as the Hindi spoken in much of India but written in a flowing Arabic/Persian script rather than in the Indian script known as Devanagari, the one where all the letters have a line on top.

(People whose first language is English often forget that in many countries, even people who aren't as well-educated as the Baigs often speak several languages, including English, in ways that make it easy for English-speakers to travel!)

Professor Baig was concerned about how poverty was becoming a problem in his village. Many educated villagers could not find work. He had four sons and a daughter who was yet to be married. He joked that he would get his daughter married once she learnt to milk a cow. He had a big house, and his family took great care of us. We had gooseberries and tea and met with people who lived in the area and cultivated fruit.

Hindu Kush: Base Camp and Mountain Views

Scenes from Town

The Trek Team: Pat and Chris are in the lower photo

Flowers in the rocks, and a view of Languta-e Barfi

Meanwhile, thirty porters were preparing for the trek. Professor Baig's son, Irshadul Haq, was our base camp manager, our cook was Hayat Ahmad, and Naseeruddin was the cook's assistant.

Our trek was to last four weeks and cost $2,000 each.

Rather heroically, Hayat Ahmad and Naseeruddin were to prepare food for the expedition during the month-long Islamic fast and time of reflection known locally as Ramzan, which overlapped with our four-week expedition.

Known in Arabic and in the West as Ramadan, Ramzan is the ninth month of the Islamic year. The Islamic year follows a timetable based on the moon. It comprises twelve months each of approximately 29 to 30 days duration, from new moon to new moon each time.

For this reason, the Islamic calendar doesn't map directly onto the ordinary sort of calendar year, which is defined by the sun's maximum elevation in the sky at various dates and thus called a solar year. Each month of a solar year falls in the same season and in the same relation to the solstices and equinoxes as the years repeat, so that December is always in the middle of winter in the Northern Hemisphere for example. The Islamic year is known, similarly, as a lunar year, a year in which the months follow the moon rather than the sun.

In most countries, the solar year has twelve months too. But the months have generally been made a bit longer in order to keep pace with the sun. Every solar year, Ramadan begins about eleven days earlier on average, as do all the Islamic months and the Islamic year itself.

In fact, both kinds of calendar are used in Muslim countries. But the solar calendar is understood to be for mundane purposes such as working out when to plant the crops, while sacred dates and important commemorations are in the lunar calendar.

From Zondrangram, it was a two-day walk to the base camp. We trekked to Duru (3,350 m). In fact, I beat all the porters to the Duru camp, and they couldn't believe it. They didn't like being outdone by a woman. But I had just done five months of hiking and was pretty fit.

We then headed to Kotgaz where we pitched our tent for the night. This was to be our base camp for the next month. The views of Languta-e Barfi and Koh-e Langar (7,070 m) were spectacular. To the west was Udren Zom (7,131 m), Shakhawr, and to the east, Saraghrar (7,349 m).

Kotgaz provided summer grazing for the village. And so, we were hemmed in by 7,000-metre mountains in the distance and cattle on the ground. I noticed the impacts of deforestation. People had chopped down trees and the bare rocks were exposed.

Pat got sick that night from the watermelon she had eaten earlier that day. But being a seasoned mountaineer and an experienced traveller, she was carrying her medication.

The men danced by the fire at the camp. One of the men had some low-grade marijuana which I tried smoking. It wasn't nice. Pat was horrified when she heard what I did, and we joked about it. The next morning, Pat and Chris left for their trek. David and I had to figure out our route.

Professor Baig visited us at the base camp and told me about the snow melt and warned that it could be dangerous. It was a good warning because I was not inclined to do anything that would endanger my life.

A climbing partner is very important for every trek. It's a relationship of trust and understanding. As Pat points out in her book, *Wind from a Distant Summit*, the right partner leads to a higher degree of success and a good climbing relationship increases the chances of survival if things go wrong.

David was an interesting guy. He was a dairy farmer and told us how he left his land in Zimbabwe and come to New Zealand. In fact, he got along well with the local people who were mostly of the Pashtun ethnic group, the second largest in today's Pakistan, and they discussed their cattle. Some of the cows were sick and they would bring their cows for grazing. People would pick herbs which were used for medicinal purposes.

Many herbs from this area have been officially recorded by the United Nations Food and Agriculture Organisation (FAO) as having strong medicinal effects: anti-epileptic, anti-diabetic, blood-pressure-lowering, cholesterol-lowering, wound-healing-promoting, possible anti-cancer activity, antimicrobial, anti-fungal and anti-viral, anti-inflammatory, good for stomach ulcers and good for the liver. In short, to employ a familiar expression, some of the old wives' tales about herbal remedies are true.

David and I had our differences. For the five days while we were to decide on our trek, David sat around the camp reading books. Finally, we went to a nearby valley to practise some of our mountaineering skills. We simply did not get on. And David didn't seem very fit. Despite this, we managed to trek as high as 5,500 metres on one of the routes to the glaciers.

We had agreed, beforehand, that we would climb to 4,800 m and camp so that the next day we could go up to 5,500 m and head back down. Unfortunately, David changed the plan unilaterally and decided to go ahead and camp at a different place. It didn't feel good, and it was difficult for me to trust him.

He reached the 5,500-metre target ahead of me and then rushed down saying it was too far and that I shouldn't bother. I didn't listen to him and went ahead by myself.

David and I were meant to go further still, but I remembered Professor Baig's warning about the snow melt. We had no satellite phones nor avalanche transceivers (or beacons, not to be confused with personal locator beacons which we didn't have either). If anything happened to either or both of us, the chances of rescue were dim.

Besides, I was carrying a very heavy tent and David hadn't brought my bivvy bag: an alternative, lightweight accommodation for sleeping in. It was going to be too much hard work in thin air to hump the tent for another day onward and upward.

But what really changed my mind about pressing on was the fact that the very day after we'd gone to 5,500 metres and back, there was an avalanche onto the section of trail we'd been on the day before!

Trekking, with David and a goat (for fresh food)

Resting – and snowy vistas

I decided I couldn't risk my life any longer, and that it was better to head back to the base camp. David, of course, never forgave me for this. But unfortunately, this was a decision I had to take, and I have no regrets. I thought about Pat and Chris and was worried for their safety as well. They were due to arrive the day after we reached the base camp, but there was no sign of them. I asked David and the cooks to look for them while I stayed at the camp by myself.

While I was at the camp, I had an interesting encounter with a middle-aged shepherd with two wives who propositioned me. He told me of his two wives who he described in less than flattering ways. He thought I was strong and then proceeded to ask if he could sleep in my tent with me. In hindsight it was hilarious, but at the time I was a bit concerned. I declined and politely told him to take his cattle to his village or I would speak to Professor Baig. Later, two shepherds came by and slept outside my tent on the rocks, presumably for my safety.

To express my gratitude, I thought it would be good to share a meal with them. I had some dried food packets that I was living on for a month – roast lamb with potatoes – that I had carried from New Zealand. We also had a green vegetable that was locally available. But then it occurred to me that sheep-meat with potatoes and a local green was probably something they ate all the time. So, I offered a fish dish, drinking chocolate and cornflake biscuits to my guests. We swapped dinner. I had their tea and bread. They loved my meal and I enjoyed myself that evening and went back to my tent and they to the rocks.

I spent almost a month in the base camp and one day it occurred to me that I hadn't come to the Pakistan to see only mountains. I wanted to meet more people and understand the culture. Two of the boys at the camp walked with me to Professor Baig's house in Zondrangram. It was a Friday, and I was asked to stay with the women in a big room. I had a long, flowing dancing skirt which I had bought in Agra. I gave it to one of the girls, but she just whipped it away. I guess they're not allowed to dance or wear flashy clothes. I showed the girls my tattoo and they were surprised. Salman, one of the boys in the house, later told me that the girls all wanted to be like me. But I must say, the girls were all educated and seemed happy. They taught me to make chapatti over a dirt fire, and I had dinner with the family.

Salman also asked me about his brother Irshadul, our camp manager. He wasn't just enquiring about Ishad's well-being, he wanted to know if Ishad was reading the Qur'an and praying, as it was the month of Ramzan. I found it a bit weird that he was checking on his brother, and there was no way I was going to tell on anyone. "Who are you" I asked, "the Muslim Brotherhood?" I slept there that night, and the next day I decided to take a jeep to Chitral. They all walked me to the vehicle to say goodbye.

It was a shared vehicle with other passengers. I was surprised to find that everyone in the jeep spoke perfect English and there was an architect amongst them. They were surprised to see me as well. By now, my scarf was back on my head. I asked them to drop me at the Tirich Mir Hotel. I relaxed that evening and had chicken for dinner. The next day I was sick – a bad bout of food poisoning which lasted for two days and two nights.

When I felt better, I decided to walk to the town to get some hair dye and Nivea cream. I didn't want to look like a bride anymore and got myself a long dress with long sleeves and a different scarf. I walked past an army scout, and he looked at me. In fact, he followed me to my hotel and informed the local administration. Soon, an armed guard arrived at the hotel and insisted he stay in my room, so I would have an armed escort. I went to the reception and told the people.

I wasn't comfortable with having some strange guy with a gun in my room and asked to see his boss. I met the head of the army scouts, who was angry that I did not want any guards.

Pretty soon the issue was escalated all the way up to the governor of the province, whom I was taken to meet! He said it was my choice if I wanted to be under armed guard, but that if my life were threatened in any way, he would not be able to do anything about it if I were without a guard. And worse, should anything untoward happen, he would lose his position and pension. With him was a man who appeared to be a conservative mullah, for he declined to shake my hand. The governor also talked about his sons who were studying in Melbourne. In the end, I didn't want to be rude, so I asked for a policewoman to be my guard. Problem solved!

I met the head of the policewomen and was assigned a policewoman called Zaina, who came from the Kalash minority, sometimes also written as Kalasha.

Zaina was thirty-three. She had been a well-known dancer when she was around sixteen years of age. I noticed that she wasn't carrying a gun.

The Kalash live in a region that is often called the crossroads of the world. While some local populations look East Asian, and others are of Indian appearance, others such as the Kalash seem more European. Thus, the region appears to have been populated in prehistoric times from the east, from the south, and from the west. Historically recorded influxes of religions and invaders have come from several directions as well.

Traditionally, the Kalash were said to be descended from Alexander the Great's Macedonian-Greek army. There is no hard evidence for that claim. But certainly, there is no doubt that this is a region where a wide variety of wandering tribes, invading armies and missionaries of different religions have all ended up.

There are affinities of language across the miles, too. Surprisingly enough, both English and the Kalash language belong to the so-called Indo-European family of languages, spoken in native terms over a vast area of Europe and Southern and Central Asia, along with more recent colonial extensions in the form of English, Spanish, French and Portuguese to practically every corner of the globe.

Another member of the Indo-European family which has been very influential in spreading its words around, via overland routes throughout southern and central Asia, is Persian or Farsi, the majority language of Iran.

Persian words pop up everywhere in central and south Asia, the most familiar being *stan* as the suffix for a name of country. Like its near-identical Spanish equivalent *estan,* the Persian suffix *stan* means 'are'. Thus, Afghanistan means 'Are Afghans' and Tajikistan means 'Are Tajiks', while Pakistan literally means 'Are Pure'.

Even Nepali is an Indo-European language, near the extreme eastern end of the family's original range; though Sherpa is not, being of the family that contains Tibetan and Chinese instead.

About half the Kalash continue to follow their own religion, which some scholars consider to be a unique form of ancient Hinduism. Followers of this old religion are notable for believing in *peri*, a Persian word for fairy-like entities who are held, by followers of the old Kalash religion, to live in the mountains and occasionally descend to the meadows.

As I mentioned in Chapter One, the Kalash are also Pakistan's smallest ethnic community; the believers in the old Kalash religion are Pakistan's smallest religious community as well. Zaina's parents were working hard to build a house. Her boyfriend was also in the police, and they were both training.

I was curious about life in the barracks, and she told me that policewomen lived in the barracks with their children. I was impressed. She also spoke about her sister who had married a Greek Orthodox guy and was hoping to get to Greece at some stage. During my tour, I had met a Kalash woman and given her some money for her children. Zaina said I didn't have to do that, but I felt bad for the children. I also had a tour guide who was a staunch Sunni and believed that everyone should accept Islam, much like the born-again Christians in New Zealand. He even wanted me convert to Islam and made several attempts, but each time I politely declined.

I was encouraged to see that the Kalash women were doing well. I visited the Bumboret Museum, which was headed by a female archaeologist, Sayed Gul Kalash. I also noticed that there were other women working in the museum and government offices. Many of them were wearing their traditional head gear, though some were wearing scarves over the head gear.

Chitral Area: Kalash in traditional dress speaking to Zaina (left), and Zaina with two men (right)

With Kalash people and Zaina

On the other hand, I also encountered symbols of ancient feudalism. We went to a castle and met the prince who lived there. He owned land and was very wealthy.

There were no land reforms in the region and feudalism festered on. There is not much access to contraception, either. On the other hand, the ancient plagues that used to keep the population down even in the absence of contraception have been tamed here, as they have in most other countries. So, the population growth is phenomenal, and the cities are booming.

Along with their rural estates, the princes and other castle-dwellers also own most of the good land in the cities of Pakistan. They consequently profit from modern urban growth,

207

even though they have done little to cause it other than by denying their people family planning.

I met another guy who was an Isma'ili Muslim, the sub-group of the Shi'a that I mentioned before. He told me the story of how polo was brought to Pakistan in 1936 by the British. Even today, an annual polo festival is held here, and the Shandur Top is known to be the highest polo ground in the world. He complained that Pakistan had become something of a police state because of terrorism and objected to the fact that he needed a pass to travel in his own country. Each time he wanted to go up the road, he had to give the pass to the police.

On the other hand, there were good reasons for these precautions. The Taliban were notoriously intolerant of religious differences, it goes without saying, and the Isma'ili were in their gunsights. In Chitral town, buildings belonging to members of the Isma'ili sect had been blown up six years before.

The town's Shi'a mosque had also been destroyed. For, the Taliban also had it in for Shi'a in general, even though the Shi'a constitute a really major branch of the Muslim religion, and not just the smaller, weaker and more easily persecuted Isma'ili community in particular.

The dangers faced by the Kalash were, if anything, even worse. Some of the Kalash are Muslims, but the ones who venerate *peri,* or who practice one or other of the 'wrong' sorts of Islam, have also suffered considerable persecution by Muslim zealots since the 1970s. The distinctive national costumes of Kalash women also fly in the face of the extremists' rather dismal ideas of what females should wear.

In February 2014, one of the leaders of the Pakistani Taliban overtly declared an "armed struggle," as he put it, against those Kalash who resisted conversion to a Taliban-approved religion.

This was reason to be fearful indeed, as the Pakistani Taliban has carried out a series of extraordinarily brutal attacks, which have not received much publicity in the West but are certainly known to the Pakistanis.

Attacks such as the Peshawar School Massacre in December 2014, the same year I was in Chitral, in which 150 died, including at least 134 school pupils and the seven gunmen themselves as the authorities closed in.

As you might expect, there seems to be no basis for that kind of atrocity in the holy books of the Muslim religion. Even on the differences of religion about which the Taliban are so obsessive, what the Qur'an says, in an English translation of a key passage, is that:

"If God had so willed, he would have made all of you one community, but he has not done so, in order that he may test you according to what He has given you; so, compete in goodness. To God you shall return, and He will tell you the truth about what you have been disputing." *(Sura 5, verse 48)*

Passages such as this have often been interpreted by Muslim rulers as meaning that tolerance should be extended to other organised religions. Above all to Christianity, Judaism and Zoroastrianism, which along with Islam have long formed a cluster of rather similar and mutually cross-pollinating faiths. But also, very often, edicts of tolerance were applied to Hinduism and Buddhism as well.

Religions that had more of the character of folklore were not granted as much respect; though, there were still strictures against forced conversion.

Injunctions to be respectful in peacetime were accompanied by codes of chivalry for times of war. Muslims are commanded never to be the one who starts a fight, and to always retaliate proportionately.

How do you get the Taliban, and ISIS, from that? It is true that these extremists wrap themselves in the mantle of religion, as did the witch-finders of Christendom in Shakespeare's day. But then again, as Shakespeare wrote: "The Devil can cite scripture for his purpose."

The late Abdur Razaq told me that despite its outward religiosity, the Taliban was "just a gang."

Or maybe a cult. Perhaps that is the best way of looking at it.

Certainly, it seems to be a general rule that cult members are indeed capable of just about any extremity.

Take, for instance, the ones who killed themselves in the belief that their spirits would ascend to Comet Hale-Bopp. It has been said that such people go crazy in groups and regain their common sense one at a time. That is if their foolishness does not get themselves killed, of course.

To date, no huge massacre has been inflicted on the Kalash. But the danger was obviously real.

25

My Isma'ili companion gave me food and perfume and seemed to have developed a romantic attachment to me. But if so, it was unrequited. I went back to my hotel and waited for Pat, Chris and David to arrive.

Pat and Chris broke the news that had not been able to summit Languta-e Barfi. They made it up to 6,130 metres and were only two hundred metres from the summit, but the weather was bad with low visibility and temperatures of minus 25 degrees Celsius. Going ahead would have meant spending the night in the bad weather, so they decided to turn back.

Pat told me that she had enjoyed herself and that they would have spent another night on the mountain, had the weather permitted. But she also says that she is not "summit-driven" anymore. In her words, as recorded by a journalist, "I relish the experience more than the summit."

That was quite a cool thing to say, for when Pat and Chris were attempting to climb it, Languta-e Barfi was only ever known to have been summited three times, first in 1963 and then twice in 1973, in all three cases from the north or the north-west. Pat and Chris would have been only the fourth team known to have summited the mountain and, of course, the first to climb it from the south.

In town, it was interesting to hear the perceptions of the locals. We had used the internet in cafés, and soon learned that word about a group of foreigners in Chitral was spreading. Which was a bit of a worry in a place that kept attracting the attention of the Taliban.

Though the Taliban didn't seem to be very popular as such, a lot of local people seemed to think that there was too much Western influence in the region, all the same.

I tried to bring up the issue of who the Taliban really were: that is to say, apart from being a gang or a cult. Some people told me the Taliban comprised five groups, and that they had not emerged out of thin air, but had shadowy backers dating all the way back to the days when the Americans first organised a guerrilla force to fight the Soviets in 1980s Afghanistan. Other alleged backers included India and China. Certainly, I know that ties with Pakistan's own security forces have also been very frequently alleged; although the children murdered in Peshawar were attending a school that was actually run by the military. Others insisted that it is in India's interest to have a destabilised Pakistan.

We also made some conversation about the neighbouring region of Kashmir, divided between India, Pakistan and China, and I heard it was easy for Pakistanis to get into the Indian-controlled part of Kashmir. They just had to bribe the Indian army. Apparently, the price was not too high; though then again, that might have just been some sort of joke!

Most of the people I spoke to agreed that they wanted a democracy and were sick of the war. While I was there, the people were also discussing how best to clear out the last dangerous parts of the Chitral Valley and make it entirely free of terrorists.

The talk of the town was a penitent Taliban veteran who had come out of the wars with four wives and thirty children to look after. Now that he had sworn off sustaining his new tribe by means of plunder and booty, he wanted the government to help support his rehabilitation and that of others like him.

I also heard of a Greek Orthodox Christian who had built a house in the area. His house was raided by the Taliban, who kidnapped him and took him away. It seems he knew that he was going to be kidnapped and had, maybe, resigned himself to martyrdom. After his fortunate release, he decided to leave the country.

On our way back to Islamabad from Chitral, we were accompanied by armed escorts once again. This time, we wanted to take a shorter route. We decided to try the Lowari Tunnel, which was then under construction (it was formally opened three years later, in July 2017). The Lowari Tunnel gives year-round access to Chitral, which is otherwise cut off by road from the rest of Pakistan, and indeed the world, in winter.

We met the manager in charge and asked him about life in the region. He told us of the dangers and how his family could not live with him for fear that they could be kidnapped by the Taliban. He treated us to cappuccino and in the end allowed us to pass through the incomplete tunnel. Pat says getting permission to go through the incomplete tunnel probably had something to do with our visitor status and the fact that we had an armed escort. She also attributes it to my powers of persuasion. Driving half an hour through a dark tunnel with wet, unsealed, rock walls was quite an experience. We reached Islamabad, where I flew out.

I was impressed with Pakistan. The scenery was breathtakingly beautiful, and the people are amongst the most kind, caring and peaceful that I have ever met. It was a tragedy to see the devastation that the war had inflicted on the region and the fall in tourism and financial support that had come about as a result. I would like to return to the country someday.

Website version of this chapter

a-maverick.com/blog/chitral-and-the-hindu-kush

Notes

Nanga Parbat attack: Taliban say new faction killed climbers. (2013, June 24). *BBC News*. Retrieved from **bbc.com/news/world-asia-23027031**

The website of Hindu Kush Adventure Guides is **hindukushadventureguide.com**. Note that it is singular in the weblink. There is a page about Professor Baig's books on the website.

Patricia Deavoll's *Wind from a Distant Summit* is published by Craig Potton Publications, Nelson, New Zealand, 2011.

On the human use of Chitral-region herbs and Pakistani herbs more generally, see Aftab Saeed, 'Medical, culinary and aromatic plants in Pakistan', accessed 2 December 2018 on: **fao.org/docrep/x5402e/x5402e15.htm**.

Regarding the Taliban commander's February 2014 declaration of "armed struggle" against the Kalash, see Agence France-Presse, 'Pakistan's polytheistic Kalash tribe threatened with death by Taliban', *The Guardian* (UK), 13 February 2014, at theguardian.com/global/2014/feb/13/pakistan-taliban-video-warning-chitral-valley, accessed 29 June 2021.

On the Peshawar school massacre, see the *Encyclopaedia Britannica* entry, at **britannica.com/event/Peshawar-school-massacre**, accessed 29 June 2021.

"If God had so willed . . .". For the source of this translation see PBS, 'Muhammad: Legacy of a Prophet', page **pbs.org/muhammad/ma_otherrel.shtml**, accessed 27 June 2021.

"I relish the experience more than the summit": In Andrew Stone. (2016, January 9), 'Battling her way to the very top'. *New Zealand Herald*. Accessed 22 June 2021 on: **nzherald.co.nz/nz/news/article.cfm?c_id=1&objectid=11 571109** .

For Patricia Deavoll's account of her 2014 climb on Languta-e Barfi with Chris Todd, see: **publications.americanalpineclub.org/articles/13201213380 /Languta-e-Barfi-South-Face-Attempt**, accessed 22 June 2021.

CHAPTER NINE

Adventures in Kashmir

A beautiful but divided land, at the western end of the Himalayas

Map detail of northern India and environs, featuring Kashmir and the location of Dharamshala, the subject of the next chapter

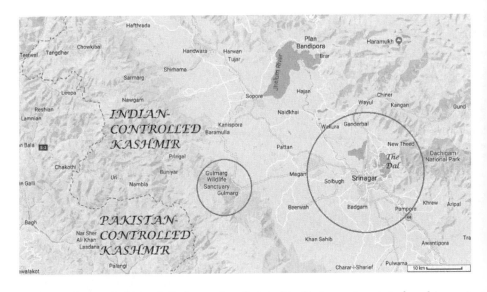

Srinagar (larger circle) and Gulmarg (smaller circle). Gulmarg is a popular ski resort, as well as a wildlife sanctuary. Background map data ©2018 Google, country names, circles and 'The Dal' overlaid

I HAD been invited to Kashmir by a local guide, who called himself Raj when he was working in the Indian capital of New Delhi but who reverted to his real name of Yaqoob whenever he was back home in Srinagar: the historic capital of the land of Kashmir.

Kashmir was another of these fabled Shangri-Las in the foothills of the Himalayas, which sounded so exotic from afar but turned out to have a lot of problems up close.

From time to time a separate country, spelled Cashmere in the English of earlier times, Kashmir was taken over by the British as a 'princely state', or protectorate under a local ruler, in the 1840s. Since the independence of India and Pakistan,

Kashmir has been carved up between them. During the war of 1962, China also bit off a few chunks as well.

Srinagar is in the Indian-controlled part of Kashmir. But the locals mostly don't seem to feel as though they are Indians, but rather as Kashmiris temporarily under foreign rule. A form of foreign rule that is in one particular sense worse than that of the British, who at least kept Kashmir, formally speaking Jammu and Kashmir, whole.

The Indian authorities regard Kashmir as a rebellious province, and the part they control is flooded with their troops, who are also there to confront the Pakistanis. As for the part controlled by the rulers of Pakistan, they call it Azad Jammu and Kashmir or Azad Kashmir for short, meaning 'free Kashmir'; though I don't know if Azad Kashmir is that much freer than the Indian or the Chinese parts of this heavily militarised and divided nation in actual fact.

In the last few decades, local discontent, moderate to begin with, has also been taken advantage of by the same Taliban elements that were sowing chaos in nearby Chitral and elsewhere in Pakistan.

And so, Yaqoob's rebadging of himself as Raj for marketing purposes in the less contested parts of India was on the one hand mildly comical but, on the other, understandable. Raj is of course just about the most Indian name imaginable; while, to Indian ears, Yaqoob made him sound like somebody from the troubled (and unfriendly) nation of Pakistan. Even if, for the moment, Srinagar is in India too.

When Raj-for-the-time-being got me a ticket from New Delhi to Srinagar, he assured me that I would love the place. He insisted that Kashmir was the most beautiful country in the world and arranged for me to stay with his cousin and brother who owned a houseboat. I flew over some indeed beautiful mountain ranges into Srinagar. There, I was met by Yaqoob's cousin and adopted brother Ibrahim and taken to a houseboat on the Dal, the city's lake.

A few facts

Kashmir is internally volatile; and there have also been three wars between India and Pakistan over Kashmir, in 1947, 1965 and 1999. Kashmir was also the western theatre of the 1962 war between India and China. Territorial disputes that began in the 19th century continue.

Pakistan controls the northwest portion (Azad Kashmir), India controls the central parts (the Indian state of Jammu and Kashmir) and southern parts (Ladakh), and China controls the north-eastern portions (Aksai Chin and the Trans-Karakoram Tract).

As befits a region located in the 'crossroads of the world', the demography of Kashmir is largely mixed, though it is more segregated than it used to be. Kashmir, narrowly defined to exclude Jammu, is strongly Muslim. Jammu, on the other hand, has a predominantly Hindu population: more so since the massacres and clearances that attended the partition of India and Pakistan in 1947, atrocities which hit Jammu very hard.

Before that date, Jammu, like many other regions on the future frontier between the two states, was more mixed.

As for the Ladakh area, it has a high concentration of Buddhists.

Much of Kashmir's economy is sustained by tourism, but the development of an anti-foreign insurgency and the abduction and killing of tourists, particularly in the 1980s and 1990s, greatly damaged the industry. Foreign governments issued travel alerts and warnings advising people to stay away from Kashmir. In 2010, the region also witnessed protests by the youth against alleged atrocities by the Indian armed forces. Curfews are common and part of the life in the region.

(I provide references for all this historical background, and for other points, at the end of the present chapter.).

Indeed, I wasn't aware that there was a curfew in Srinagar from 9.00 p.m. onwards till I got there. I was also told not to venture around the city area and the mosques, the so-called 'security areas' on a Friday.

Plus, getting a SIM card for my phone was impossible. I had to borrow one from Ibrahim.

Arriving and staying on a houseboat

The houseboat itself was really quaint, though, and I was provided with breakfast, lunch and dinner. The Rough Guide to India advises tourists not to get stuck on a houseboat at the mercy of a dodgy operator. They ask you to stay onshore and explore the area for the ideal houseboat. But quite frankly, I wouldn't have wanted to stay in the small town. It wasn't attractive, there were people and dogs everywhere, and it was quite dirty.

There were intricate wood carvings and silk carpets on my houseboat. But in contrast to the houseboats that ply the backwaters of Kerala—a state of southern India that I also visited around this time, where houseboats move around in the sheltered waters behind the shore—I found that on Srinagar's Dal, the boat was stationary. What with the curfew and the boat's stationary nature, I was confined to narrow and unchanging quarters at night. That was the only problem I had with the houseboat I stayed on while in Srinagar.

Ibrahim was a very nice host. We talked about the recent storm that had had such terrible effects in Nepal, and also destroyed many villages and caused people to be marooned for days together in Kashmir. In Srinagar too, houses were waterlogged; and the government took time to get its act together. I also sensed a bit of the Kashmiri anger against the Indian armed forces. One afternoon, I was at an internet café in town busy doing my work. Suddenly, one of the guys working on a computer turned around, and said, 'We are under occupation.' I didn't have the time to get into a conversation. I looked at him sympathetically, and said, 'I'm sorry about that.'

Indian armed forces (top); Narang Temple (below)

Srinagar: The Dal (City Lake). Woman gathering herbs in middle photo; Ibrahim at bottom.

Pir Panjal (top) and Hari Parbat fort, Srinagar (bottom)

Narang

Narang

In Tahawaz

The Western Himalayan subalpine conifer forests are quite special

A house in the wilderness, subalpine conifer forest, and the Thajiwas Glacier

Later that day, I took a shikara tour around the Dal. Shikaras are small boats, much like gondolas with canopies. Most houseboats have their own shikaras which guests can use. The placid, eighteen-square-kilometre Dal or City Lake, with its reflection of the Pir Panjal mountain range, is a big draw for tourists. The Dal has numerous sites of interest – an early morning floating vegetable market, the floating gardens where lotuses bloom in July and August, and Char Chinar, the famous landmark island on the lake. A number of other gardens around the lake are also accessible by shikara.

I had read about the famous fort and mosques and was keen to look around. I found an auto-rickshaw driver, a young local Muslim man who took me around. The driver lived as an artist in New Delhi during the winter, and, in the summer, he said he earned about $300 a week driving his auto-rickshaw in Srinagar. His English was great, and the armed forces let him into most places.

The ancient fort of Hari Parbat was our first stop. This fort was used by the armed forces because of its strategic location and had been closed to the public for the last twelve years. The local tourism department had, lately, succeeded in having it partially re-opened.

The fort was begun by the Mughal emperor Akbar and was later completed by a Pashtun ruler, Shuja Shah Durrani in 1808. Inside, there is a temple, mosque and a gurudwara (Sikh house of worship). Hence it is place of worship for Hindus, Muslims and Sikhs, when they can get in.

The fort is built on a mountain and can be viewed from any part of the city. The Hindu section was well maintained, but the Muslim section was not in use as yet. Electronic speakers to relate the history of various parts had just been installed, as they had done in some forts that I had lately visited in Delhi. I really enjoyed exploring the parts of the Hari Parbat fort that we were allowed into.

We stopped next at the Khanqah Shah-e-Hamdan Mosque, also known as the Khanqah-e-Moula. This was a most beautiful mosque--although strictly speaking if a mosque is the Muslim equivalent of a church, a khanqah is more like a chapel or traveller's prayer room. The website SrinagarOnline says that khanqahs are "often found adjoined to dargahs [Sufi shrines] and mosques," and that the stand-alone khanqah in Srinagar is only "popularly known" as a mosque.

Originally built just prior to the 1400s CE in honour of the Persian Sufi pir (roughly, saint) Mir Sayyid Ali Hamdani, the Khanqah-e-Moula has been burnt and rebuilt several times and today remains an architectural landmark in the city.

The Khanqah-e-Moula is a square wooden building, adorned with carvings on doors and windows, wooden mouldings, and magnificent chandeliers. As a non-Muslim I was not sure if I would be allowed in. The SrinagarOnline website says, in mid-2021, that the Khanqah is restricted to Muslims only. But fortunately, I was allowed in when I visited.

Like many other Muslim houses of worship, the Khanqah had special women's prayer areas.

Khanqah-e-Moula, Srinagar. The interior decoration is in painted papier-maché, a characteristic Kashmiri art. This khanqah was founded in the 1300s CE, and is currently built in what seems to be a mixture of East Asian and middle Eastern styles.

Khanqah-e-Moula

My next stop was the Jamia-e-Masjid, the main mosque of the Srinagar area, where thousands of people gather for Friday prayers. This mosque forms a quadrangle around a fountain garden with gatehouses on four sides. It is known for the three hundred and seventy wooden pillars of its courtyard, each made from a single deodar tree. Though it is in the bustling old town of Srinagar, the Jamia-e-Masjid is silent and peaceful all the same.

Jamia-e-Masjid

Jamia-e-Masjid (top and left; note the wooden pillars, 370 in total); Hari Parbat fort (right)

The third mosque I went to was called Ziyarat Naqshband Sahab. This is actually a mausoleum and also houses a graveyard. It is open to people of all faiths. While I was there, there was a body and people were praying. I apologised to the woman praying for taking a photograph before I realised that it was a funeral, and she said, 'Oh no, we are happy. She is with God in heaven now, she is alive.' And I thought, what a wonderful feeling. And it really felt like some of the Catholic churches in the south of Spain. I don't believe in any particular religion, but I did feel a spiritual energy in some of those mosques.

Jammu and Kashmir form a popular tourist destination for Indians. Many come to Jammu on pilgrimage and others come to the Kashmir Valley to experience the scenic beauty. The alpine peaks, snow-capped mountains and green meadows are a regular backdrop for Bollywood films. You find many Indians taking that mandatory touristy photograph, all decked up in Kashmiri garb against the beautiful scenery. In fact, the Indian tourists were spending more than the backpackers. I was told that the backpacker market in Kashmir is not very encouraging. The reason is probably because backpackers can't easily get travel insurance for travel in this area.

I had heard that Kashmir was a popular skiing destination and decided to make my way from Srinagar to Gulmarg. The big attraction here is the lift that takes you to a height of 4,000 metres where you can get a great view of the mountains. The ski season is from December to March, and temperatures are well below zero. There was some skiing happening while I was there even though it wasn't the skiing season. There was a light snowfall and most of the people were Indian tourists. What shocked me was that not horses, but Kashmiris were dragging Indian tourists on sleds. This was surely not a good look in a disturbed and secessionist region!

Ibrahim was very eager to get me to go out on a multi-day tramp. He had a lot of guides who didn't have work. Generally, the trekker took a mule and I thought that would be interesting, but I just wasn't keen to go by myself. Probably because it was the end of the season. It looked really good, and I would have loved to go out in a group, but there was no way I was going to pay $200 a day, and that's what put me off. When I was in Pakistan, it was $500 for a week, not $200 for one day. The cost aside, I thought the glacier was absolutely beautiful. The snow-capped Thajiwas Glacier looms over Sonamarg and makes it really picturesque. We drove all the way to the base of the glacier. On the way, I saw the huge camps of the Indian armed forces. They had a rock-climbing wall, presumably to train the soldiers for warfare in the region.

I did do a trek from Narang up to the Gangabal Lake, which was a good 3,350 metres. Narang is a tourist village known for its scenic beauty. It is also a base camp for trekkers to Gangabal Lake and Mt Harmukh. The scenery was amazing with alpine slopes and snow-capped mountains. I also saw the ruins of the Wangath Temple Complex, which was built in the eighth century CE.

After this, I went back to Srinagar and took a jeep down to Jammu. It was a beautiful drive, but you could see the camps of the Indian armed forces. I got some beautiful Kashmiri scarves. At Jammu, I was meant to get the bus to Dharamshala (also spelt Dharamsala in English), a city famed as the abode of the Dalai Lama in exile; but the bus I was on went all the way down to Manali, so that was annoying, and I had to get a taxi to Dharamshala.

Later on, in 2016, Yaqoob came to New Zealand, and we went trekking together on Mounts Tongariro and Ruapehu in the central North Island of New Zealand. There's a photo of Yaqoob in another of my books, *A Maverick New Zealand Way*.

Website version of this chapter

a-maverick.com/blog/adventures-in-kashmir

Notes

On Kashmir's political volatility and wars see, for instance, 'A brief history of the Kashmir conflict', *The Daily Telegraph, Monday,* 24 September 2001, retrieved from **telegraph.co.uk/news/1399992/A-brief-history-of-the-Kashmir-conflict.html**

On the three-way partition of Kashmir, see 'Kashmir: History'. (2012). In *The Columbia Electronic Encyclopedia (6th ed.).* Retrieved from **infoplease.com/encyclopedia/world/kashmir-history.html**

On the balance of religions, see 'Jammu & Kashmir: Distribution of Religions' (n.d.). Retrieved from kashmirstudygroup.com/awayforward/mapsexplan/religions.html

On dodgy houseboat operators, see *The Rough Guide to India, 9th ed.* (2013), **roughguides.com**, pp. 468, 471.

Regarding the Dal or city lake in Srinagar, see **travel.india.com/srinagar/places-to-visit/lakes-dal-lake/** and also 'Dal Lake' in *Wikipedia*, **en.wikipedia.org/wiki/Dal_Lake**.

On Hari Parbat Fort, see the entry on the website 'India Mapped', retrieved from **indiamapped.com/monuments-in-india/hari-parbat-fort/**

On the Khanqah of Shah Hamdan in Srinagar, also known as the Khanqah-e-Moula, see the entry on **SrinagarOnline, srinagaronline.in/city-guide/khanqah-of-shah-hamdan-in-srinagar**

On the Jamia-e-Masjid. see the feature in *Tour my India.* Retrieved from **tourmyindia.com/states/jammu-kashmir/jama-masjid.html**

On the Ziyarat Naqshband Sahab, there is a useful Wikipedia entry: **en.wikipedia.org/wiki/Ziyarat_Naqshband_Sahab**

CHAPTER TEN

Dharamshala

The Dalai Lama's current home address

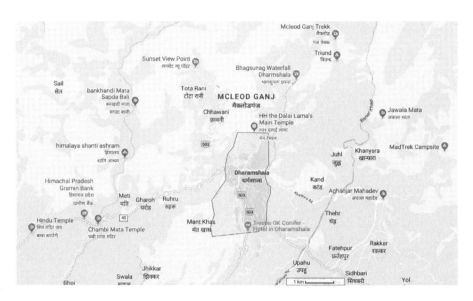

Dharamshala and environs, including the suburb of McLeod Ganj where many Tibetans live, and His Holiness the Dalai Lama's Main Temple. Map data ©2018 Google.

MY trip to Dharamshala had its share of twists and turns. The wrong bus from Jammu had landed me in a hill-resort town called Manali, which was pleasant enough but not where I was planning to go. A seven-hour taxi ride later, I finally reached my destination.

Dharamshala lies just south of Jammu and Kashmir in the present-day Indian state of Himachal Pradesh, of which it is the winter capital (Shimla is the summer capital). Dharamshala is internationally famous as the long-term base of the Dalai Lama, who has been exiled from Tibet since 1959.

It was November and the tourist season was over, but the town was still crowded. I had read up about the history of Dharamshala. The city was for a long time located within the princely state of Kangra, ruled by the Katoch dynasty.

After the British annexed the state, keeping its ruler on the throne and ruling it at arm's length as they did in many such cases, they raised a military regiment from its population; a regiment which came to be known as the First Gurkha Rifles and which is now part of the modern Indian Army. Many of those soldiers fought in both World Wars.

Dharamshala would have become the summer capital of British-ruled India but for an earthquake in 1905 that caused widespread destruction. Today the city is famously known as the home of the Dalai Lama and the Tibetan government in exile.

The Kangra-Katoch arrangement lasted until the independence of India, after which Kangra was dissolved into the modern Indian state of Himachal Pradesh.

I had heard the story of the Dalai Lama's escape from my guide back in Manaslu. It was a sad story of how the Chinese government bloodily cracked down on a Tibetan rebellion in 1959, in which many thousands of Tibetans were killed and about two thousand Chinese troops as well. The Dalai Lama, then a young man, escaped to India on foot, trekking for fifteen nights to escape the Chinese troops. He was granted asylum in

India and permitted to stay at McLeod Ganj, a suburb of Dharamshala which is also referred to as 'Little Lhasa'. Many Tibetans followed the Dalai Lama and made Dharamshala their home. Others who fled Lhasa have settled in Nepal and Bhutan.

The Dalai Lama has been able to draw the world's attention to Tibet's fight for independence. Gaining the Nobel Peace Prize in 1989 made him even more famous, particularly amongst Western audiences.

There have been several Western novels and films about Tibet: a country which has an exotic reputation at a distance, like all the other Himalayan nations. James Hilton's 1933 novel *Lost Horizon*, which was later made into a film of the same name, drew attention to the Tibetan cultural realm in the form of Shangri-La, a harmonious utopian kingdom in the Himalayas where people were happy. These days, Shangri-La, also spelt Shangri La, is a familiar expression in the English language. I've used it already in this book without explaining where it came from, till now.

Another film, *Seven Years in Tibet,* starring Brad Pitt, described the relationship between the Dalai Lama and Heinrich Harrer, an Austrian mountaineer, during the Chinese invasion of Tibet in 1950.

(The Communist Chinese army, which had just expelled the Nationalist Chinese from the mainland to the island of Taiwan in 1949, only captured a small part of Tibet in 1950. All the same, it was clear that they could take over the rest of Tibet if they wanted to, and so the invasion led to the signing of a treaty under which the Dalai Lama became a client of Beijing, until the 1959 uprising and crackdown made his position entirely untenable.)

In 2004, a Tibetan music album, *Sacred Tibetan Chant: The Monks of Sherab Ling Monastery*, also won a Grammy award for the best traditional world music album.

It was a special experience. I have always been fascinated by Tibetan culture. As I have related, I had tried to go to Tibet but couldn't get into the country.

All the same, I had the special experience of being blessed by the Dalai Lama while he was on a visit to New Zealand. And this time I was lucky to encounter the Dalai Lama once again, as he was in McLeod Ganj. He was speaking at his monastery, and I went to listen to him. The gathering was very crowded, but it was interesting to watch how people welcomed the Dalai Lama and the way they revered him. Being in the crowd and listening to the Dalai Lama speak was an experience and his presence was awe-inspiring. I stayed throughout the speech and listened.

I love how the Tibetans dress. They wear a robe-like long wrap dress over a shirt held together by a belt at the waist. It's called a Chupa. Underneath it they wear trousers or additional layers of skirts to keep warm. Married women wear multi-coloured, horizontal-striped aprons. The dress also varies from region to region. The monks, however, dress in a long, maroon wrap skirt with a yellow shirt and a maroon scarf. They shave their heads in accordance with their religious traditions of austerity and simplicity. You can see the Dalai Lama dressed in a similar fashion as well.

Dharamshala

Buddhist monastery (top) and temple, Dharamshala

Dharamshala: Gate to Tsuglangthang complex in McLeod Ganj (top); Tibetan National Martyrs Memorial (below)

Inside the Buddhist temple, Dharamshala

Dharamshala lies in the most incredibly hilly terrain: a bit like New Zealand's capital city of Wellington, only more so. McLeod Ganj, which means McLeod neighbourhood, is about five hundred metres, more than one and half thousand feet, above downtown Dharamshala. The British, who founded Dharamshala in the mid-1800s, treated the town as a refuge from the summer heat – the name Dharamshala means a house of rest in Hindu tradition – and I suspect that McLeod Ganj was even more of a getaway for them. The suburb was named after a governor of the Punjab named Sir Donald Friell McLeod. I do hope that a highly flattering depiction with halo and cherubs never went to the old Scotsman's head!

'If only the wee folk back home could see me now . . .'. Or so one suspects Sir Donald Friell McLeod might have thought upon observing this saint-like depiction of himself surrounded by what the modern online caption describes as "admiring Sikh elders," Wellcome Collection, [UK] Science Museum Group, photo No. V0048411 via Wikimedia Commons, CC BY 4.0.

In addition to being the Tibetan part of town, McLeod Ganj is also where the backpackers tend to hang out. You find many Western tourists staying in small cheap rooms in the lanes of this quarter, or volunteering at the Tibetan NGOs. Many expats have also settled here more permanently, opening cafes and inns for foreign tourists.

Some people also come to McLeod Ganj to study Buddhist philosophy, meditation, and yoga. A few tens of metres downhill from the main town square in McLeod Ganj, just before the dizzying plunge into downtown Dharamshala, is the Tsuglagkhang complex. The Tsuglagkhang is a Tibetan Buddhist temple, the largest outside Tibet itself. It has a huge meditation hall with interesting murals depicting Lord Buddha in various forms. Outside you can see the multi-coloured Buddhist prayer flags fluttering in the breeze. People practice the ritual of walking clockwise around the temple praying. And there are prayer wheels too.

The monks often stage open debates here. I have read about it. It seems that a monk preaches about an issue and the rest of the crowd sit around and roll their eyes and try to mock and intimidate him. It is all done in good humour! That would have been interesting to see, but I'll have to wait until my next visit.

The Tsuglagkhang complex also houses the small Tibet Museum, organised around an interesting and well-documented permanent exhibit of the Chinese occupation and the struggle of the Tibetans. There are photographs and blood-stained clothing of Tibetans said to have been held by the Chinese as political prisoners and tortured. Outside the museum is a memorial to the Tibetans who died fighting.

The museum is not just for non-Tibetans, but for the local Tibetans as well. It represents the history of their struggle, an important reminder for the youth. You can see the Tibetan flag on many buildings in McLeod Ganj. Known as the snow lion, the flag has become a symbol of the Tibetan independence movement and is strictly banned in China. The complex also has a small bookshop with several books written by the Dalai Lama.

From the temple I headed to the much-talked-about Bhagsu or Bhagsunag waterfall. This is a regular haunt for the tourists in addition to being a sacred site, but I wasn't very impressed with it as the flow of water was only a trickle when I was there. That was the result of dry weather and the taking of its headwaters, which are obviously not so sacred as all that. Lack of flow is now a big issue at Bhagsu, which is only guaranteed to be a proper waterfall complete with mist and spray during the wettest weeks of the monsoon season. There were some monks dipping their clothes in what holy waters remained, and tourists taking photographs on the rocks nearby.

On the southern edge of the downtown area, the HPCA (Himachal Pradesh Cricket Association) Stadium is another attraction. At an altitude of 4,110 feet or 1,256 metres, roughly the average altitude of downtown Dharamshala as a whole (McLeod Ganj being another 500 metres further up of course), the HPCA Stadium is supposed to be the highest international cricket pitch in the world.

The backdrop of the Dhauladhar range, part of the so-called Lesser Himalaya Range (still 6,000 metres or so), makes the stadium especially interesting. In 2013, the sports journalist Andy Wilson wrote that:

"A cricket ground where a bowler can accurately be described as running in from the Himalayas end is clearly an unusual addition to the international circuit. . . . Worcester it isn't."

The downtown is quite crowded, and you may want to escape to quieter parts, including McLeod Ganj, and observe the majestic Dhauladhar range. Or, trek to Triund. I've heard a lot about the trek. The route takes you through oak, rhododendron and deodar forests. There are small tea stalls along the way for those wanting to take a break. The last kilometre, with some twenty-two curves, can be a challenge for inexperienced trekkers. But the view from Triund is amazing – the Dhauladhar range on one side and the Kangra Valley on the other. I have seen photographs and it's definitely on my to-do list.

Dharamkot seems to be another popular getaway spot. I heard of inns tucked away in the forest without any drivable roads nearby, and you either trek or take a pony ride.

Returning to McLeod Ganj, guidebooks describe the suburb as a food heaven – pizzas, lasagnes, cakes and desserts, and herbal teas. I mainly loved the yoghurt and the sugar-free and gluten-free Tibetan food.

In some ways, McLeod Ganj reminded me of Kathmandu – busy and crowded, but peaceful.

The preservation of their traditional art and culture is of great importance to the Tibetan inhabitants of Dharamshala. The Norbulingka Institute is working to ensure the traditional heritage is being sustained. They have educational training programmes for students, artists and painters. Twenty students are admitted every year for this free-of-charge residential programme that goes on for three years. The curriculum includes history, literature, medicine, poetry and religion. There is also an art apprenticeship programme where students are trained in thangka painting (Tibetan Buddhist religious paintings), wood carving and statue-making. You can walk around the studios and watch the artists at work. The Norbulingka Institute complex also houses a temple with a 14-foot statue of Buddha made by the artists.

It was a short trip. I made my way to the tiny Gaggal airport from where I was to depart on Air India to New Delhi. The flight was delayed for hours, but I met many amazing people. I made friends with a lady who was a teacher in Afghanistan, and we talked about the situation in that country. She said half her class was dead and some of her students were fighting the war. She herself had narrowly escaped a bomb attack. She said she was training teachers in Dharamshala. I also met people who had been on yoga retreats for a month. I made so many Facebook friends in that airport. Dharamshala has a special place in my memory and is one of the places that I definitely want to go back to.

Website version of this chapter

a-maverick.com/blog/dharamshala

References

Casualties in the 1959 Tibetan uprising are documented in 'China/Tibet (1950-present)', a webpage of the University of Central Arkansas, at **uca.edu/politicalscience/dadm-project/asiapacific-region/chinatibet-1950-present/**, accessed 29 June 2021.

The quote about the cricket ground is in Mike Selvey et al, 'The most beautiful cricket grounds in the world – in pictures', *The Guardian*, 25 January 2013.

CHAPTER ELEVEN

Mixed-up Mountaineering Guides

Time for another me-too movement in the hills?

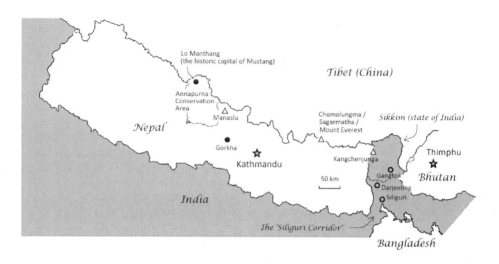

Nepal and its immediate neighbours. India is shown as grey.

HOW does it feel when your guide says he wants you for a second wife? On the day you depart for a 23-day hike that includes summiting two mountains — Island Peak and Mera Peak — which are both over 6,000 metres high? Well, this is what happened to me in April 2018, on my third visit to the Khumbu region of eastern Nepal where Everest Base Camp, the Three Passes and Sagarmāthā National Park are all located.

On day one, he smells of alcohol and you think, maybe he just drank too much the night before. You just keep making excuses like that at first. After all, he was my Facebook friend for one year and came recommended by a French mountaineer (what on earth was that mountaineer thinking?)

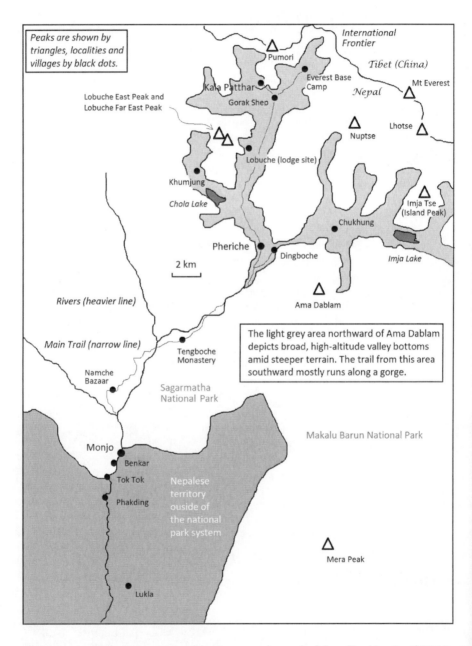

Back to the Khumbu again (and hoping to scale nearby Mera Peak), April 2018.

Here I am with my guide in Kathmandu on the 21st of April, before the fun started!

My guide told me that he had summitted each of Imja Tse (Island Peak) and Mera Peak about eight times. He was holding his accounting book showing how much he made. But I soon noticed that no one seemed to know him anywhere, and hotel

257

managers told me there was a problem with my guide, pointing their fingers to their heads.

Then, he never offered to take a photo of me. It was me doing selfies the whole day long.

On the first day, I walked ahead of him from Lukla: 'I'm fitter than he is!'

On the second day, he said he could catch up.

I have a rat phobia. I had paid $4,000 to summit two mountains and stated that a condition of my expedition was rooms with no rats.

We arrived in Phakding at the end of the first day and there was a rat in the roof: no sleep that night! He panicked and searched out other hotels while I just slowly made my way to Namche Bazaar.

We arrived for the second night in Namche Bazaar, and he wanted me to stay in a dark dingy hotel behind the renovations taking place on the Buddhist stupa. I said no, I was not staying there, and made my way to the Sherpaland Hotel, where I stayed the last time I was in the town.

He argued with the hotel management, and with me, for two days. I went to the hotel he had picked and got a refund. The manager told me the cost was $25 per night. The Sherpaland was $35 per night, but I got the last room.

The other guides came up and told me that there was something wrong with my guide: that guides are meant to stay with their clients and order their food. My guide did not even stick with me on the trails.

In this collection of photos, I am flying out of Kathmandu, landing at Lukla, inspecting the welcome sign at Tenzing-Hillary Airport (Lukla), and hiking to Phakding, with the main photo a Buddhist prayer wheel at Phakding

Stupa under repair at Namche Bazaar

As it turned out my guide did not like the dorm-like sleeping arrangements at Sherpaland, I stay in dorm-like conditions from time to time when backpacking around Europe. At least the rooms are warm.

I said to the owner of another firm, please train your grand-daughter to be a sherpa guide. He said he did not have a grand-daughter, and that woman belong in the kitchen!

Well, as I later found out, the company my guide came from had female guides for female clients. But unfortunately, I hadn't got one!

There are lots of wire suspension bridges on the trail, including an very high and scary one officially known as the Sir Edmund Hillary Bridge. If you are coming from Phakding, this bridge is the last bridge to cross before you get to Namche Bazaar: with about another two hours' walk ahead before you actually get to the town.

The high bridge was erected a few years ago, above a now-decaying bridge built, I believe, in the 1960s with the help of Sir Edmund Hillary, and also known as the Sir Edmund Hillary Bridge in its day.

The old bridge is still there. But I don't think anyone is supposed to use it now.

The new, high bridge was already in use when I first hiked this section of trail.

The trail and its bridges are used both by trekkers and porters, and also by local people moving goods on yaks, dzos and mules. The resulting traffic jams can get dangerous given that the trail and its bridges aren't very wide.

This collection of photos was taken further up the trail. The new Sir Edmund Hillary Bridge is in the middle row, at the left

In Phakding, I got to know an Australian woman. When she was crossing the new bridge before Namche Bazaar, a yak attacked her with its horns and almost pushed her off. Her friend in the group saved her.

This time around, I made a point of trying to get to the new bridge by midday, since four-footed animal traffic tends to build up in the afternoons.

I made sure there weren't any potentially unruly beasts in sight when I crossed.

Anyhow, my guide said that the new bridge was seven months old. Which really made me wonder whether my guide had ever crossed this bridge, I knew the place better than him! Was this some kind of scam, or something?

After Namche Bazaar, I thought things could not get worse. The next day we went on to Tengboche. I chose a hotel named Tashi Delek, where it turned out that none of the staff knew my guide.

He thought he had to sleep on the couch in the dining hall; but guides were given their own rooms! He said he had stayed there seven times. Yet the common story everywhere was that no one knew him.

Our porter stayed at the porter house, where the arrangements were just mattresses on a floor in a warm building. This was more communal than the private rooms for guides, though they got great food. Had my supposed guide only been to Tengboche previously as a porter?

From Tengboche, which is officially at 3,867 metres elevation, we were going to Chukhung (a bit of a hike, which would take seven hours and one that would gain about 900 metres in additional elevation.

We were going to go via a village called Dingboche, which sounds like Tengboche but is a different place, further up the hill, at 4,410 metres.

My guide said his leg was playing up. He said that he could not walk properly and that he would go slowly. He then blamed me for going too fast the previous two days, i.e., getting to the Namche Bazaar bridge to avoid crowds and yaks.

It was snowing when we left Tengboche, and I spoke to a Sherpa woman minding ten yaks. She was going to the village of Gorek Shep (5,164 metres), near Everest Base Camp. Gorak Shep is so high up that it is not occupied in winter. I asked why she was not a mountain guide, if she hiked all the way up there and back: her job did not have to be in the kitchen.

It snowed every day. The visibility on the way to Chukhung was going to be really bad.

The Everest View Hotel, Tengboche, and the view from my window at sunrise

In Dingboche, we stopped in at a café called Mama's Bakery and had the best momos ever, even though Dingboche was pretty much in the middle of nowhere. Momos are a kind of local dumpling, which is a staple food. Mama's Bakery adjoins a guesthouse called the Green Tara Lodge, which is owned by Yahjing, a lovely lady from Namche Bazaar, and her husband Tashi. Yahjing told me that Tashi was Tibetan, a former Buddhist monk, and that they had married thirteen years previously and had two children.

Mama's Bakery

(The name of the lodge looks Irish to Western eyes: but in fact, the Green Tara is a spiritual figure in Tibetan Buddhism.)

I visited the toilet, and it was so clean that I thought I would stay at the Green Tara Lodge on the way back down, if it wasn't full. I was attracted to the unusual cakes in Mama's Bakery: for instance, a garlic, lemon and ginger cake! And, to the Tibetan flag on the wall and the Buddhist altar.

My guide went through to Chukhung very quickly. I met so many other trekkers throughout the whole way who were concerned for my welfare. Several people had commented that 900 metres in one day was dangerous and that to do a peak within six days of my arrival in Nepal was even more dangerous. Which is to say, that such rapid ascents risked altitude sickness.

My guide said this was fine and was no problem: but he just appeared as an imposter. He got to Chukhung by 1 p.m.: what had happened to his bad knee, and why the erratic behaviour?

Anyhow I met this amazing English guy who was carrying his father's ashes. His father was a mountaineer who had been at least part of the way up Everest and had died ten months previously. The Englishman and his wife were meant to be doing the Base Camp trek to Everest, to spread his father's ashes at the Base Camp.

But his wife had become pregnant with their second child, due on his father's birthday, and so she wasn't able to go all the way. He freaked out about the date coincidence: I said it was normal and I had known other people who this sort of thing had happened to.

He was helpful, and I walked with him for about an hour.

He was recounting his fathers' descriptions of the track, from memory. What an amazing goodbye.

From Tengboche to Dingboche, Mama's Bakery, and then on to Chukhung: note the low-lying cloud on the way up

Then I met a couple from Poland, who took a trip once a year for two weeks without their kids; then took a trip once a year with their kids.

They were breathless getting up the hill to Dingboche and we walked together for two hours. I was to meet them later at

Mama's Bakery, and we also shared a helicopter together on the way back to Kathmandu, all by chance.

The couple were staying the night in Dingboche: so, onward and upward to Chukhung by myself. I had paid $4,000 for a guide recommended to me by a friend in France, and this guide was nowhere to be seen, having gone on ahead of me.

I got lost out of Dingboche as the visibility was poor, with low cloud and sleet. I almost wandered off the track and up a hill instead and had to ask porters and ordinary Nepalis how to get to Chukhung.

The vegetation was sparse, and pregnant yaks grazed on the new Spring growth.

My guide sent the porter to find me at 4 p.m. I was staying at the Sunshine Eco Lodge in Chukhung. After I had arrived a Singaporean tourist asked, in what was now becoming a familiar mantra, what is wrong with your guide? The Singaporean's name was Siri. His guide was amazing: he ran around, got the food, and asked if Siri was ok. Never once did my guide ask if I was ok: it was all about his knee, followed by a blister.

Siri's guide had maps, and they discussed the trail, about the precise route they should take up the Island Peak Summit. My guide had no map, no drinking bottle (he borrowed mine) and no sufficient snow gear. He and his brother owned the agency I had hired him from: ironically enough, an agency that seemed to have lots of other bona fide guides.

I was really wanting to trust my guide to take me to the top of Island Peak. He said he was Nepali and did not need a drinking bottle- so he just drank mine! I noticed our porter, a man called 'D', was really tired. So, I fed him for the next two days.

The owner of the lodge told me not to talk to people, or to talk so loudly, which I thought was a bit much. Then he charged me $80 for hiring boots and other equipment. Siri only paid for one day: I paid for two days hire to be on the safe side.

I decided to leave the Lodge abruptly when I was told I could only wear the mountaineering boots from Island Peak Base Camp: a three-hour walk up and another 500 metres in elevation. I had put my orthopaedic insoles into those boots and could not easily take them out and use my hiking boots as it taken an hour to put my insoles into these mountaineering boots. After this insult, I left early for Island Peak.

(One guide was living in a tent outside the Lodge, and he told me it was so cold!)

The room my guide initially booked me into was dark and dingy and I asked for a better room. The only difference was that the covers on the bed were cleaner. There was mould in the walls and another guest complained that the water froze in her drinking-water bladder.

I had stayed at a better hotel in Chukhung on my last trip, and just did not like the mould: you get sick. And on top of that, the owner was a control freak telling me not to talk to anyone!

I had hoped that relations with my guide would be more convivial on the way to Island Peak Base Camp, as we were now in what is technically known as Very High Altitude terrain.

At this elevation the risk of succumbing to altitude sickness (an illness caused by lack of oxygen in the blood) or to some other danger is so great as to leave little room for error. Proper acclimatisation is the most vital precaution, and on average it is necessary to acclimatise to any altitude over 2,500 metres. The danger goes up exponentially after that. Tengboche is at 3,500 metres, roughly speaking, and Chukhung is 900 metres higher. Island Peak Base Camp is at roughly 5,100 metres.

In the early 1970s, about one in five hundred trekkers in this area used to die, mostly from altitude sickness or some related problem. That's *trekkers*: I'm not even talking about serious mountaineers going higher still. These days it's very rare for anyone to die of altitude sickness on the trekking routes, but only because people are more aware of the issue and of how to tell mild cases from more serious ones.

The most usual symptoms are wheezy lung symptoms. They go from being like a cold, to being like the flu, to being like pneumonia, to being dead. The brain may also swell up as well, a particularly serious complication. It's thought that about half of all Himalayan trekkers get the milder forms of altitude sickness. If things get serious a person may start coughing up blood. And if a person does start coughing up blood, this is (as always) a bad sign.

To avoid getting altitude sickness, or to limit its likely severity if you do get it, a person has to ascend in stages, like a diver coming up from a great depth. Proper acclimatisation to Himalayan altitudes takes many days of slowly pushing higher and not overdoing things. There is also a medicine called

Diamox, though of course it's better not to get sick in the first place.

So, while common enough in its milder forms, altitude sickness is no joke because it has plenty of potential to get worse, especially if people ignore the early mild symptoms and keep pushing on. This doesn't have to be upward. Over-exertion on the level can also make a borderline case get worse.

For instance, on the way, we saw a female member of a Russian party slide down a hill. Her friends gave her water and urged her to continue. She was like a leaf in the wind even with her Nordic walking poles, and was at least 100 metres behind her group. Was she fully acclimatised? I don't know.

The trek to Island Peak Base Camp was an up and down walk, mostly up (some 500 metres). High winds and sleet alternated with sunny intervals during which I took photos. We made it after three hours, eventually.

My tent did not close properly, and I was pleased to have two single mattresses to sleep on for extra warmth. Pheasant- or partridge-type birds were everywhere, males and females pairing up for mating.

My guide told me that they were danphe, a species of pheasant which is the national bird of Nepal. So, I took pictures of them as well.

Birds are common even at very high altitudes in the Himalayas, and this is particularly true in the breeding season. They go higher in order to be safe from predators who might otherwise be attracted by their courtship. Birds' respiratory systems are more efficient than that of human beings and other mammals, which struggle to follow the birds to these altitudes.

On the way to Island Peak Base Camp with porter 'D'

More photos of the way to Island Peak Base Camp with porter 'D'

Darwin and the Danphe

The danphe is perhaps the gaudiest of all pheasants. It is Nepal's answer to India's national bird, the peacock. It's a toss-up which is the more spectacular. To my mind the danphe looks like a magical bird from the pages of a fairy tale. The danphe is the avian equivalent of Joseph with his coat of many colours.

273

A male specimen of the Danphe or Himalayan Monal, national bird of Nepal, which we did not get to see. 'The Beautiful Himalayan Monal — Male on Snow. In Tungnath, Uttarakhand'. CC-BY-SA 4.0, image by Ajit Hota, 2017.

Well, the male looks like that. As with all pheasants the danphe hen is a drab creature, much harder to spot. Nature intends it that way, of course. Among heavy, ground-living birds of the pheasant type, it's vital that the females do not attract the attention of predators. The less well-camouflaged males are presumably more expendable.

The less gaudy pairs of birds I photographed, not danphe presumably

Though it makes evolutionary sense that the females of big birds that live close to the ground should be harder to spot than the males, the exceptional gaudiness of the male in many species of pheasants, peacocks, and chickens was a poser for Charles Darwin.

He could understand how it made sense to have a well-camouflaged female and a moderately showy male, as with ducks. But how did it make sense for the males to be even more flamboyant than a drake (i.e., male duck)?

Why should heavy birds that lived close to the ground do everything possible to draw a predator's eye? And to encumber themselves with a great big heavy tail as well, in the case of the peacock?

In the end Darwin concluded that the females of these species must have an eye for beauty that trumped all other considerations; perhaps because gaudiness was also a signal that the male in question was healthy and vigorous.

And so, the hen mated with the male who most caught her eye even if he also caught the eye of the tiger a bit later: with every successive generation of males becoming a bit more conspicuous than the last.

Whether this kind of evolution could go on indefinitely was a good question. In fact, it didn't seem that it could! Like the antlers of the stag, which served a similar function, the peacock's tail obviously could not keep on getting bigger, forever, simply to please the peahen or, in the case of the stag, the doe.

So, maybe in some cases evolution *didn't* always favour the survival of the fittest; at least, not in the long run. Maybe in some cases evolution more or less got side-tracked by mate preference The result was such improbable-looking creatures as the peacock, the danphe and the stag.

Today, we would say such creatures have a place in nature that is like that of a red sports car in a stream of traffic. Practicality and safety have been sacrificed in favour of showing off to the females. And nature has proven as willing to make this expensive choice as some men have.

But the courting pairs we saw were drab in both sexes, the products of a more mundane form of evolution: the family-car variety one might say.

In other words, they weren't danphe. Actually, I think they were Himalayan snowcocks, or possibly Tibetan snowcocks: species that are related to the danphe but in which both sexes are drab. Which begs the interesting question of why males should be gaudy in some species but not among their relatives!

A Pattern of Errors

Only later would I discover my guide's misidentification and realise, in the same instant, that it fitted into a wider pattern of unreliability. He didn't even get Nepal's unmistakeable national bird right. So, what else was he wrong about?

Anyhow, at Island Peak Base Camp the toilet was overflowing. It reminded me of similar sanitary problems at Gorek Shep, near Everest Base Camp, which people sometimes call Gorek Shit.

I was invited to have dinner at 6 p.m., which was noodles. I refused as I am gluten intolerant. My Pringles chips came in handy and so did my Snickers bars, as I had purchased three of them. I had to sing out for boiled rice instead of noodles.

The Singaporean trekker Siri, who I introduced in a previous instalment, was at Island Peak Base Camp with his guide as well.

We would be leaving to climb Island Peak, more properly known as Imja Tse, at one a.m.

My sleeping bag was frozen at one in the morning when we prepared to leave. I had tried to do an equipment check earlier, at the Hotel Sherpaland back in Namche Bazaar, but my guide spoke to someone else on the phone, and never checked my equipment.

Even the night before the climb, my guide had refused to check all my gear. It now turned out that I was missing an additional drinking bottle or a bladder that could take hot water, necessary in the high Himalayas as cold water would freeze. I didn't have enough for the two of us. What a disaster.

The root of this problem lay in the fact that the hiking gear I had assembled in New Zealand had gone missing on an Air Canada flight from Montreal to Toronto. After a 24-hour flight from Toronto to Nepal via the USA, I tried to buy all the most essential mountaineering gear I needed in Kathmandu in one day, before leaving with my guide. But clearly, one or two things were forgotten.

At 4 p.m. we made it to Crampon Point, where I discovered that to make things worse still, and in fact hopeless, one of the drink bladders that I did have had been unsuitable for filling with hot water and had burst.

And so, we turned back to Base Camp at 4 a.m., arriving at 7 a.m. The Porter 'D' was collecting my bag at 10 a.m. from Base Camp, so I repacked that. We then went on our way to Chukhung. I was not going back to the hotel. Instead, I made my way to Dingboche. I put my orthopaedic insoles into my hiking boots and wore them.

I went into Mama's Bakery and the Green Tara again to stay the night. This time around I got to meet Yahjing's husband Tashi, the former Tibetan monk. I loved meeting Tashi: what a character. My guide did not have to pay to stay here. He had his own room but had to pay to house and feed the porter.

At Mama's Bakery. Myself on the left, Tashi, and Yahjing on the right

That night, my guide told Tashi that the Dalai Lama was mad and should not follow the Americans. Tashi said that Buddhists do not get into fights, so he got up and left instead. I thought my guide should have been the one to leave the table.

The next day I had coughing fits and was even coughing blood. I also felt as though I really needed to rest. These were grave signs of altitude sickness, probably the result of our racing ascent to Island Peak Base Camp.

According to the itinerary my guide had drawn up, we were to have climbed Island Peak (6,189 m) on my ninth day in Nepal, after only seven days in the mountains. As it turns out, this was too soon by the recommended standards, whereby the final attempt on such a peak should be left until people have spent about two weeks trekking slowly higher and higher towards it. It's easy to be wise in hindsight about such things. But of course, that is what guides are meant to be for.

Goodness knows what would have happened if we had not been so short of water to the point of needing every last drop and if one of my water bladders had not then burst. For we would have pressed on to the summit, roughly a thousand metres higher still. And then I might have been overcome by altitude sickness and not been able to make it down, which is another worst-case scenario and a factor in many deaths on Everest and other high mountains.

Mountaineers say that getting to the top is the easy part. It's coming down when you're stuffed and quite possibly suffering from altitude sickness that has come on during the climb that is the hard part. And of course, you have to get down under your own steam or you will die. That is, barring a rescue which isn't likely to succeed at Himalayan altitudes and puts other people at risk anyway.

Back in Dingboche (and really, we should have been lower still in view of my condition), my guide was overheard outside the bakery saying he wanted to change hotels. He asked me if he could save money by having the porter share his free room. I said he should come to some financial arrangement with Tashi all the same. I told Tashi, but he never charged.

Tashi was a great storyteller. We had monks visiting the bakery-cum-lodge, and at night Tashi talked about how at age twelve in 1985 he had escaped from Tibet, riding in a truck that crossed over the Indian border.

Tashi said that young Tibetans these days had forgotten their culture and smoked and drank and rode motorbikes.

However, the Dalai Lama ran Tibetan schools that enjoyed some degree of tolerance from the Chinese authorities. Tashi hoped for more autonomy for Tibet. The present Dalai Lama has predicted that he will live to be 113 years old and will witness such a development before his demise.

Tashi's own surname was Lama, which means Priest. And it turned out that my guide's great-grandfather came from Tibet as well.

My guide liked Yahjing and Tashi's momo dumplings, too. But his behaviour seemed erratic. Tashi offered free meditation and other help to guests and made a point of extending this offer to my guide as well.

I warmed to Tashi, who took pity on my guide and treated him with compassion. The next day we were going all the way to Namche Bazaar, so I chose a small hotel run by a friend of Tashi's. I wanted to keep the peace, but I knew I had to finish this expedition somehow. My guide was weird, and I had to leave.

When we made our way back to Namche Bazaar after leaving Dingboche the next day, my guide said we should buy land together. And I said: "No Way!" Why would I?

In Namche Bazaar, we stayed at Tashi's friend's place, the Lasha Hotel, which was small and not used to putting up guides. I could hear my guide talking to the family all night and I thought: 'Oh dear, what an imposition on them'.

That morning on the downward rocky path, full of people, yaks and porters, I told my guide that I wanted to finish the trip and that it was over with.

He somehow managed to get thirty porters agitated with his response.

I also said I would not have any congratulatory dinner with his family, and that I would not be going to his house to eat, sleep or be his second wife.

Monument to a female Sherpa guide under construction in Namche Bazaar

I thought I could get some money back but, no, I would get nothing back.

An Australian family came over and asked whether I was OK. They said that I could trek with them for the day. Thanks Tim, Edith and Jasper! You came to my rescue at a time when I did feel very much under siege. And after the 30 porters were agitated, I did feel very unsafe on that track.

My guide had screamed at me and said that I should finish the trip and I would not get any refund of any kind. I thought my guide was going to hit me, or that a porter would bump me off the track.

Later that day the monsoon which normally comes in summer, arrived early. The daily snows of an unusually protracted winter promptly turned into daily rains. The fine spring weather known as the climbing season never eventuated. Hillary and Tenzing wouldn't have made it up Everest in these conditions! Was this a consequence of global warming?

I had tea in the porter house, though my guide said the porter had been busy and had four kids. He personally had only one kid and was not busy. I was free, and would I sleep with him? I said nothing but decided that this trip was definitely off.

That night, I got to Phakding and found my hotel. My guide stayed elsewhere and peered through the windows, which seemed rather weird. Though, I was getting used to weird by this stage. Once again, the manager of the hotel contributed his assent to the general judgement that my guide was weird.

My guide and the porter 'D' spent the day drinking masala chai which was normally quite expensive but provided for free by the hotel under the custom whereby guides get things free. Eventually the hotel manager chucked them out.

The manager had only one guest and that was me. Flights from Kathmandu had stopped for about three days, which was serious. Because of the ruinous climbing season, hotels had next to no guests.

Is this a portent of things to come? Will the climbing season change to October and November? Last year it was warm then, and there wasn't much snow.

This isn't just a concern for climbers. If less snow were to fall in the Himalayas, the rivers in India and Pakistan would become less reliable in the drier parts of the year, affecting the agriculture that feeds hundreds of millions.

Next day, I put the fact that my guide had wanted sex on my Facebook page. I knew his wife and brother would be watching my page and I made it public. I got to Lukla by myself. It rained all day.

At 3 p.m. I went to the Danphe Café, where my guide had previously taken me on the way through and introduced me to a so-called owner (probably a friend of his), who had met us there and taken the permits, thus boosting my confidence in the climbing enterprise.

This time, on the way down, I discovered that the people in the Danphe had never heard of my guide (and they were all Sherpas).

So, it seems my guide had arranged to meet a friend there on the way through who did not work at the hotel; pretending to own it when he did not. What a web of deception. I could simply not keep up with it.

I found another hotel. I fell down the steps near the airport. Two Irish ladies picked me up and we sat down and arranged a plan of action. I was to get my own hotel and go to the Tourist Police.

My guide had gone off with my luggage. I texted him and said he had fifteen minutes to come over, or I would go to the Tourist Police. After fifteen minutes I went to see the Tourist Police. They checked the date we came through in a book full of tourists' and mountaineers' names. (I was surprised at how many seemed to come from the Ukraine!)

The Tourist Police officer who was helping me check the register had a photo of his son and his wife on his mobile. He said he was from another town nearby. Most men in Nepal love their family: just not my guide! That's one thing I love about Nepal, myself. In the middle of a crisis, we talk about his family and his people: just love it.

The Tourist Police rang my guide. He came down and started yelling at me. A crowd gathered outside the post. I had had enough of listening to my guides lies and yelled back.

The friendly Tourist Policeman then called his bosses. About 4 guys came down and listened to me. They said they did not want guides like this in Nepal. My guide was drunk and smelt of alcohol, something the Police picked up on (they noticed it before I did).

They said the fact he took off with my bag and that I had no hotel meant they would punish him. I took them back to my hotel. The senior police officers, a guide a porter and a manager from the Namaste Lodge, who were all there, all said that some women were even being raped by their male guides, and this had to stop.

All women deserve to be treated with respect. This sort of thing also happens in other countries. Do not get me wrong — I'm not having a go at Nepal.

The guide this story is about was my third guide in the Himalayas so far. I have had problems over warm rooms with others, and my second guide refused to take me up Island and

Lobuche Peak after I paid a whopping $6,000; he also stated that I did not know how to use crampons. I complained to the New Zealand embassy in India. Nothing was done about this, nor the guide censured in that case.

This time I was asked to get married, sleep with the guide, and buy property. The only answer as far as I am concerned is to have a female guide next time. Several guiding companies in Nepal offer female guides: you can go online and find out.

The most professionally advanced is Dawa Yangzum Sherpa, the first Nepalese woman to obtain a prestigious qualification from the Swiss-based International Federation of Mountain Guides this January after about fifty men from Nepal had done so. Other female guides are up and coming.

Anyhow, I needed to get back to Kathmandu.

I had a ticket booked on a later fixed-wing flight out of Lukla. I wasn't able to change it and paid extra to fly out by helicopter.

The manager from the Alpine Lodge in Lukla most helpfully came to the airport at 7 a.m. and booked me onto the flight.

Amazingly, to top it all off, I then learned that my guide had used my fixed-wing ticket to fly to Kathmandu.

In addition to going to the Tourist Police once back in Kathmandu, I sent a letter of complaint to the head of the Nepal Mountaineering Association as well.

Lukla helicopter departure

With the Tourist Police in Kathmandu

Eventually, before I left Nepal, I learned from the Tourist Police in Kathmandu that my guide had suffered the penalty of having his guiding license suspended for two months (he did have one, after all). He had to report to the Tourist Police once a week to discuss respect for his craft, his wife, Nepal, Buddhism, and the Dalai Lama.

There are lovely people in Nepal, that's for sure. People who do their best to make up for the failings of others. Things would be even better if they didn't have to.

Website version of this chapter, in four blog posts: a link to the first one follows:

a-maverick.com/blog/mad-mountaineering-guides-me-too-part-one

Two YouTube videos

On trail congestion, I shot a video on one of my visits to Nepal which makes the point, and you can watch it on YouTube at **youtu.be/IdAKeMxT-ls**.

You can watch a video I shot from the helicopter out of Lukla, which gives a fascinating view of the hills terraced for farming, on YouTube at **youtu.be/Rp-YqcfxwPI**.

CHAPTER TWELVE

Batons for the Beasts

I saw tigers, elephants and rhinos in Nepal's Chitwan National Park

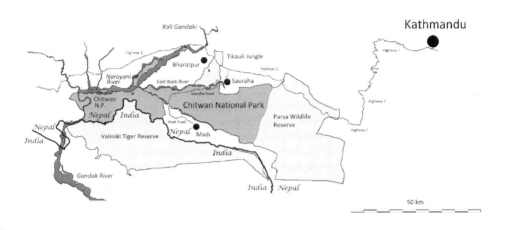

Chitwan in relation to Kathmandu and the Indian frontier

THE ride to Chitwan from Kathmandu, only eighty kilometres (fifty miles), took five and a half hours along almost-impassable roads, mainly used by slow-moving fuel tankers.

Chitwan is in the low-lying plains of Nepal, a completely different area from the Himalayan districts or even Kathmandu, which is at 1,400 metres above sea level. Chitwan is a thousand metres lower, and that helps to explain the slowness of the road down from Kathmandu.

The Chitwan region lies on the border with India. It is dominated by a vast meandering river with various names,

291

including the Gandak in India and the Narayani in Nepal, where it is also known as the Kali Gandaki. Several tributaries join the main river in this area in ways that lend it yet another name, the Sapti Gandaki or Seven Gandaks.

The confluence of all these rivers makes the whole area lush, a miniature version of the Amazon. It doesn't dry out and get dusty while waiting for the monsoon, like much of the rest of the Indian subcontinent. This mini-Amazon of the Chitwan is one of the last refuges of the tiger, both on the Indian and the Nepalese side, and that was what I had really come to see!

The Narayani arises in the Annapurna region of the Himalayas, where it is known, exclusively, as the Kali Gandaki. It is one of the most important rivers in Nepal, and its Indian leg is a major tributary of the Ganges.

The Kali Gandaki of the Himalayas has the distinction of running through the deepest gorge in the world by one measure, in the sense that it is roughly three times as deep as America's Grand Canyon as measured from the peaks of the Dhaulagiri massif on one side and the Annapurna massif on the other, to the floor of the gorge. Everything in the Himalayas is on an incredible scale!

The Kali Gandaki is older than the Himalayas. As the Himalayas rose up, so the Kali Gandaki wore away its immense gorge, though not quickly enough to escape being lifted skyward as well.

Anyhow, like an old friend, the Kali Gandaki links my Chitwan adventure to the Annapurna trek, if only by the coincidence of having the same river running past both.

Nature scenes near Sauraha

Booked to stay in Chitwan National Park

I'd gone online and booked several nights' accommodation in Nepal's Chitwan National Park, a renowned wildlife area full of tigers, elephants, and even Indian rhinoceroses (yes, there are such creatures!).

When I got there, I was glad I'd booked accommodation inside Chitwan National Park. The town of Sauraha, the northern gateway to the park where I stayed on my first night, was a bit rough. On the other hand, Sauraha enjoyed scenic sunsets over the East Rapti river, one of the local tributaries of the Narayani. The first morning I was in Sauraha, I saw elephants being ridden along the street as well! I've got a video of that on my YouTube channel, and I give the link at the end of this chapter.

As the sun climbed higher, the temperature soared past the mid-30s Celsius and was unbearably hot at times. This part of Nepal is not the Himalayas!

A hazy sunset at Sauraha

Amazing leaf patterns in the trees at Sauraha

Shopping for a Guide

I shopped around several agencies seeking a guide, as I had become extremely suspicious about guides by this stage. By the same token, if you book through a company, the guides themselves can be left with essentially nothing. And either way, accommodation can be poor. People I met were annoyed that they were paying $100 a day and being made to stay in places that surely cost no more than $2.50.

Sometimes you do not know until the last minute who will be your guide: a bad move if you are by yourself.

Basically, you want to be able to interact with whoever it is that is going to be your guide, before you take them on.

A bad choice of guides also happened to me in New Zealand. I had someone referred to me who did not have his guide qualifications; someone who wanted to take hallucinogenic drugs on the way up a mountain. I think I have had it all.

A Nepalese Safari

The hotel I'd booked to stay within the park was called the Jungle Safari Resort. The guide offered by the hotel was really nice and cost me $300, though they could not assure me of seeing a tiger. I guess tigers must just do their own thing, after all.

I loved the hotel's garden and staff and the older gentleman who owned the place. It was quaint, and my room was large and amazing, with air conditioning to keep me cool.

I did a half-day jungle safari ride on a jeep, which felt rather cramped. We took a long and very slim canoe across the East Rapti river. We saw a rhino mother and its offspring, along with three other adult rhinos and two sloth bears, a creature I'd never heard of before.

A baby Indian rhinoceros in the water

Unlike African rhinoceroses that have two horns, the Indian rhinoceros, the type found in Chitwan, has only one horn. Its scientific name is *rhinoceros unicornis*: though I think if this species of rhino ever contributed to the legend of the unicorn, the kernel of truth at the heart of the legend must have been greatly embellished.

Everybody thinks of Africa as the place where remarkable wildlife is to be found. A lot of people don't realise that many 'African' animals such as elephants and even rhinoceroses also live in India and the adjoining countries such as Nepal. Or, that the Indian region has some distinctive creatures of its own, such as the tiger (of course) and the sloth bear, which I'm going to talk about a little further on.

A Bengal tiger in Chitwan National Park. Photo by AceVisionNepal77 (2012), CC BY-SA 4.0 via Wikimedia Commons.

There are also freshwater 'mugger' crocodiles in the local rivers, and gharials as well. The gharial is a species of crocodile with a weirdly narrow snout that lives on fish. Sadly, it is almost extinct in the wild. Chitwan National Park has a Gharial Breeding Centre, whose staff are doing their best to restore the numbers.

A gharial in the Chitwan National Park's Gharial Breeding Centre – you can just see the narrow snout

Anyhow, what's this sloth bear thing, then?

Well, it's a kind of bear that wound up being named after another animal because the European naturalists who first encountered them, around the year 1800, thought that they were Asian relatives of the giant prehistoric ground sloths lately discovered in American fossil beds. Those were slow-moving, solitary, vegetarian animals that had huge claws for self-defence. They were able to fend off sabre-toothed tigers and grizzly bears but succumbed to early hunters.

The naturalists were wrong, but on the other hand, the sloth bear is indeed not your average bear.

It is a bear, but at the same time fairly unusual, with a diet that mostly consists of termites. Its babies often ride around on their mother's back as though the sloth bear were a possum — or a sloth. The babies of all other species of bear trot along beside mama bear (I'm sure you've heard how you aren't supposed to get between them). Fear of the tiger leads the sloth bear to keep its babies extra-close and to maintain a ferocious quality typical of other bears or the extinct ground sloth, even though it mostly lives on termites.

Indian Sloth Bear with cubs in Daroji Bear Sanctuary, Karnataka, India. Wikimedia Commons image by Samadkottur, CC BY-SA 4.0 (2007).

The closest I got to a sloth bear: I think you can just vaguely see it.

What else did I see? I saw the amazing colours of kingfishers, flycatchers and giant hornbills (wow, the bird life!), two monkeys, and a crocodile farm.

It was a pity that I also felt half-dead physically, with my burnt lips from strong sunshine in the Himalayas where I'd just been, and a chest infection which was also down to my recent hardships at altitude.

The next day I got antibiotics to deal to the chest infection. I'd nearly lost my voice. I had to get better.

Down at the river, after my canoe-ride, I spoke to cigarette-smoking and drunken guides, who said I should hire them as other companies used them on contract. That didn't really suit me.

I had read some disturbing stuff on Trip Advisor. I always check this out when I arrive at a place: what to do and where to go. But it's only one source of information.

The Elephant Breeding Centre was privately owned. It did rides with up to four people on the top of the elephant on a square ringed seat. The elephants were trained; but wild and domesticated elephants sometimes went crazy.

A male elephant had killed a woman, and a tourist saw it all. She said Ronaldo (the elephant) was going for her. My guide later told me Ronaldo was a wild male elephant who had broken down all the electric fences in the breeding centre. The elephants there, which were mostly female, had to be chained up. He had mated with them and produced several calves.

Ronaldo had killed several people in fact and had twice broken into fruit shops and eaten the fruit.

The people from Sauraha are very resilient as, in addition to rogue elephants, the area is visited by floods in each monsoon season. Recently, the restaurants, a baby rhino and a mother elephant were washed away. The mother took a month to die a very painful death. The mother's baby was adopted by another elephant and the baby rhino, which survived, was adopted by the people of the village, who let it eat some of their crops.

It suddenly rained, and at five a.m., off I went to the river to see what I could see. I thought 'I am not paying $22 for a 30-minute walk, up the riverside', a fee another guiding agency had sought to charge.

I bumped into a guide who was staring through binoculars. He said he preferred this to sitting in his office, and all the gambling with cards that happens around town. He would walk seven times a day to see what was going on.

A thoughtful guide, and more about the elephants

Eventually, I met a guide named Kamal whose laid-back and honest nature appealed to me. We walked and talked for about two hours, and I gave him a 50% deposit on the spot to do the tiger-watching tour (though I would pay for my own food).

Kamal said he almost got attacked by Ronaldo while with an elderly couple. He made them hide behind at tree while he lit a cigarette. He reckons anything to do with fire makes elephants run away.

So, that's how Kamal got rid of Ronaldo. Kamal also told me that in some places, elephants are only fed 100 kilos of food a day and they should be fed more. Instead of living until eighty, they die much younger.

Local private elephants were brought from India. Kamal said that having four people on their backs, and the steel seat that was also used, were cruel. He didn't mention the breaking-in process which meant they are kept in a pen for two years and broken in by their master.

Some of the other elephants were government elephants, used by the Nepalese army. These elephants were not used for giving rides to members of the public: just transporting army personnel. They seemed to be more well-fed and better looked-after.

Government elephants used by the Nepalese Army

I mostly ate out at local restaurants and the food only cost the equivalent of two dollars or thereabouts. Kamal and I continued to meet at certain times to walk along the river. I said I would depart for the town of Madi in three days' time, when I felt better.

I went to the elephant bath and refused to take a ride or scrub them with a pot scrub. At the time I thought the pot scrub made their skin go white. Later I found out that this was a natural consequence of ageing, but it still seemed harsh to scrub the elephants.

Feeding the elephants

So, I decided to feed the elephants instead of riding on them; especially the one that arrived with the steel seating. It looked tired and two old, overweight men were riding on it.

Afterwards, the people fed the elephants bunches of bananas, which was great to see. Some people were putting water on the elephants, which were relaxing, and not scrubbing them at all. Some people now pay to walk with the elephants and not to ride on them.

305

The elephant I fed had an open wound on its head. Apparently, the trainer struck it to make the elephant submit to his directions. I never saw a woman on an elephant, interestingly enough.

Another thing I noticed was that only the government elephants had tusks.

If through education people like me can feed and not ride the elephants, hopefully other people will do so also.

I could have stayed by the river for longer. But it seemed like party central; and I was in no mood for that, as I was ill. Next time I will stay by the river. I liked eating at the places next to Kamal's office. The people were genuine and really wanted to talk to you. The Everest Region, where I had been, just seemed a bit more commercial, and I was glad to be here in Chitwan, to get well and feel better.

The History of the Park

Chitwan National Park was established in 1973, partly at the expense of the Tharu people who lived there. The Tharu displaced by the park's creation number ten to thirty thousand.

I was to witness clashes over different types of survival — conflicts between locals and the army, animals versus humans — and to ask: do they have to be mutually exclusive?

In Chitwan, there are currently 650 rhinos, 250 tigers, and a number of leopards that I didn't catch.

They'd had zero poaching for the last few years, probably because there was now a battalion of Nepalese soldiers stationed in the park to protect the wildlife. There had been shoot-outs with poachers four years before, but nothing lately.

Before the king was assassinated in 2008, and a republic proclaimed, the remaining locals had policed the park. Where I went next, to the town of Madi, I found that the local people were still nostalgic for the idea of their own force.

Homestay in Madi

Madi was on the southern edge of the park, very close to the Indian border, outside the park but inside an administrative buffer zone. There is a similar buffer zone on the northern side of the park. Before 1973, Madi had apparently been a prosperous base for hunters and safari expeditions. But eight resorts had closed down since then.

When I encountered it in 2018, the town struck me as the poorest I had been to apart from Manaslu in the Himalayas. I really did wonder about the quality of the accommodation. I was worried about my health and decided I was not going to overdo things and be careful where I stayed.

So, we got a bus eventually and found ourselves going on a rocky road past two army checkpoints to Madi where I had a homestay booked.

The bus ride was a nightmare, with three people attempting to squeeze onto two seats. Kamal prevented a woman from sitting between us; she was younger than me and no way was I was going to let her share.

I was really worried as to whether I could handle this homestay situation. I had never chosen to do this before; but then it could not be as bad as the crappy hotel rooms various guides had put me in on the Everest trail.

Anyhow the accommodation was very clean, and the woman running the homestay, named Sarita, turned out to be nice. Her husband had left her to start another family seven years earlier, and her parents had bought the place. She had two married sons on the property, her sister, two nieces, her parents, and two grandchildren. And me.

With guide Kamal and scenes from the Madi homestay

Sarita's house was in a village that was part of the wider Madi conurbation, itself really a collection of villages. Sarita's village was made up of houses that all had thatched roofs. There were young children and buffalos in the streets, and dogs running around.

I had a cute hut made of mud, with interesting windows, spaces between the sticks, and a mosquito net. That was just as well. Quite apart from the mosquitos it kept out, I was grateful that it would probably keep animals at bay as well. A small mouse was nibbling on the thatched roof. I figured it wouldn't be able to get through the mosquito nets and run across my face in the middle of the night, which was the important thing.

We arrived at 11 a.m. and walked to the old temple of Shiva, where two women from Pokhara had built a house. They had sold their land in Pokhara, all in the name of karma and wanting a better life. It was so hot, and I was drinking water like there was no tomorrow: six litres in one day, all carefully treated with pills. How would I survive tomorrow's trek?

Kamal was very knowledgeable. He had been a guide since 1995, after being in the police before that. We also engaged a local guide called Oppo who was in fact Sarita's son. He was 27 and just married, very shy, but knew where the tigers were.

The whole village had moved to a new location about five years before, as another wild elephant, not the same as Ronaldo but another one, had killed about half a dozen villagers. I wasn't sure whether the relocation had been officially demanded, or whether it had happened because the old place was now thought to be unlucky.

The villagers also had to house their buffalo at night, as the tigers came for them otherwise. The buffaloes seemed to have better accommodation than the people. The local people slept outside as it was way too hot to sleep inside, other than in an airy hut.

Some of the local villagers caught fish in the river. The army tried to convince them not to. I saw the people fishing on my first night in Madi, till the army caught them at it.

That night, Sarita's mother and other women from the village were also out gathering ferns, to extract the edible insides of the stems. They did this weekly. It was a tasty vegetable and supplemented a very limited diet. The locals would also graze their buffalo near the park in the dry season, as the river ran low. This often led to conflict with the army, too.

At night the children played until 9 p.m. around the different homestay cottages and the households of Sarita's family group. Sarita or another woman would cook and serve the guests. More people would go into the homestay kitchen to cook the meals. Each household had its own kitchen; each was separate from the homestay cottages.

Two young women had been raped by the army. Sarita had a meeting with the village women about this. But the guy they accused was only transferred.

On the Tiger Trek

The next day was going to be a tough one, a twelve-hour trek from 6:30 a.m. till dusk, to Tiger Point and back. Tiger Point was the area where tigers could most easily be seen, even if a sighting wasn't absolutely guaranteed. Most of our route was along the river.

The trek to Tiger Point, with elephant grass and lots of rivers

We were given some sticks which, at first, I thought were walking sticks; but it turned out that they were batons to fend off enraged wild animals. We were told that a sick or injured tiger could attack you at any time, though they were supposed to be wary of humans otherwise. You could also be caught in the middle between fighting rhinos. I couldn't help wondering what use a baton would be in a situation like that.

We saw a tiger after only two hours on the trail, at 8.30 a.m. We had stopped to talk to some other guides and their two guests. Kamal saw the tiger first, then me too. Wow, I could not believe it: an actual Bengal tiger in the wild. The rest of the day we followed the river and Oppo let me wear his open jandals. I was going from mud, to water, to sand, and this repeated itself about thirty times through the course of the day. I had flat feet and bunions, but it seemed my feet were up for it. Oppo must have spent about five hours up a tree looking for tigers that day, by the way.

There were about eight people in the park at that stage looking for tigers. It was over 40 degrees Celsius, and the river water was really hot where it formed stagnant pools, actually too hot for anyone to swim in it! Kamal came across about ten different tiger footprints, but no other visitors in the park had seen tigers that day. I was so lucky.

Occasionally there would be wind to cool us down. But mud, sand and river water, and up banks, is what we did for twelve hours.

The army came through with elephants, en-route to their outpost in the jungle. Unlike private elephants, the army elephants were allowed to eat foliage on their way through. I snuck into a cooler part of the river for a swim and the army nearly saw me. Kamal said he did not want them to become jealous. It was funny lying in the river knowing a tiger or a leopard could come down for a drink. It was only later that I thought about crocodiles, too.

Wild jungle skies

Eventually we stopped for lunch by a cool watering hole, where the rhinos fight each other. I heard one snoring. I was told they could run at any time and to get out of their way if that happened. This watering hole was uncannily cold: it must have been fed by an underground spring or a cave-stream.

The day really was very hot, and I needed to rest in the shade every two hours.

The other tourist staying at Sarita's establishment when I was there, a Belgian guy named Leo, saw nothing. But Kamal's last two clients came within a metre of a tiger!

I loved the fact that we walked along the river both ways. Another guide joined us, saying that he would do this and do that, if he were in charge of the park. He would fix up the lookouts and also cut the elephant grass that grew everywhere—tall, bamboo-like grass common in the tropics, and in places like Chitwan—so that the tigers could be seen more easily. Of course, that would also make it harder for the tigers to hunt, so they would probably die out.

Kamal said this guy was head of his guides' association; that he took fees and did nothing with the money, apart from come up with improbable schemes like the proposal to trim the elephant grass. He wanted his subs back.

I got another restless night's sleep with the heat.

Back to Sauraha by ambulance and jeep, then Kathmandu

The next morning there was no traffic on the road. Kamal joked that there was a bus strike. In fact, a bomb had gone off at a supermarket in the nearby city of Bharatpur at a quarter to four in the morning.

The device had been tossed from a motorbike by a faction of Communists that had at one time waged a civil war against the old monarchy. The damage was limited, and nobody was hurt. The incident seemed to be more an exercise in showing the red flag than an act of terrorism. But the scare put the region's bus services out of action for the day, all the same.

So, the Belgian's guides arranged for a safari jeep to come all the way from Sauraha to give us a ride back. But the army would not allow the jeep through, as they did not allow jeep safaris in that part of the park. It was all a bit of a Catch-22.

So instead, believe it or not, we got a ride with an NGO-sponsored ambulance to meet the jeep at the checkpoint beyond which it had not been allowed to come. That was a cool ride back.

The NGO ambulance

I got back to Sauraha, stayed the night, and got the bus to Kathmandu at 7 a.m. This time around it was a ten-hour ride up the hill, as opposed to an eight-hour ride down. Still, I was feeling better. I only had a sore throat now, one that could be sorted by aspirin. Then I would be right to return to New Zealand!

Website version of this chapter, in two blog posts: a link to the first one follows:

a-maverick.com/blog/batons-for-the-beasts-a-nepalese-safari-in-chitwan-national-park-part-one

My Sauraha elephants-in-the-street video:

This is on **youtube.com/watch?v=rx-YlbWS_dc**

Conclusion

AT the beginning of this book, I said that I'd hardly known a thing about the Himalayan region before heading there for the first time. After three trips, the people that I met in the beautiful mountain ranges of the Himalayas had helped to enlighten me. The cultures, the histories, the landscapes and the environment were truly inspiring, and I felt humbled by the friendless and the willingness of people to let me into their lives and share their stories with me. Beyond my culture shock, I found some of the most wonderful people on earth.

From the rugged peaks in the Hindu Kush through to Sikkim, I was amazed at the similarity of the landscapes. To trek the whole thing in its entirety would take three months, and it is something I would like to do one day – yet another addition to my bucket list. While I was there, I met people who had walked for three months straight along the rugged baseline of the vast mountains. I found that the more I saw and the more I learnt, the more things I wanted to do and the more I wanted to accomplish.

I was amazed at certain areas in the mountains where I discovered religions and belief systems that were so different to one another yet were practised and celebrated side by side every day. There were people with an interpretation of Buddhism which is completely different to Buddhism in Korea and Japan, and there are the different Muslim traditions. And I found some cultures were more musical than others.

I learnt that while these people are so unlike other cultures I have encountered, at the end of the day, everyone wants food on the table, a happy community and a healthy environment. It's the simple needs that form the invisible links between us – the need for shelter, warmth and a harmonious existence in our given surroundings.

The people of the Himalayas are very self-reliant and resilient. The way in which the different communities come together, especially in natural disasters like floods and earthquakes, is something we should all take note of. Their dedication to the land and their religions, however different, was intriguing, especially for people who often live hard lives in even harsher environments. In one of the world's harshest environments comes a tantalising, colourful and inspiring collection of cultures and people – amongst the snow, the wind, the rocks, and the yaks.

The beauty of knowledge there is what got me – the understanding of medicines and flowers – which showed the ancient traditions and shared belief systems tracing far back through interconnecting histories. The knowledge that they still had based on ancient findings and teachings was fascinating. Each culture shared the common medicinal knowledges based on the plants of the Himalayas and developed unique cultural traditions related to the immediate environment.

The rivers flowing from the Himalayan snow melt give people, land and the animals in all the surrounding countries fresh water. The water that runs through the Ganges, for instance, is considered some of the most sacred to the Hindu people; it is an important part of Hindu religion and culture across India, yet it too comes from the Himalayas. I think the area of the Himalayas truly shows how people and their environment become interdependent on one another. I enjoyed every minute of it and would love to go back and visit the areas I have not yet been to.

Acknowledgements and Thanks

Thank you to all the trekking friends, guides and porters I met along the way, those who have shared moments of their life with me and become a part of my experience of this world.

I want to thank my friend Yaqoob, who invited me to Kashmir and also showed me around Delhi and central India as Raj, and became a friend.

I would like to thank Sampo from Pokhara; my first personal guide in Nepal, and also my friend.

Additional thanks are due to my editor Chris Harris, and to everyone who checked my manuscript along the way.

Thank you to everyone for listening.

Other books by Mary Jane Walker

Did you like *A Nomad in Nepal?* If so, please leave a review!

And you may also like to have a look at the other books I've written, all of which have sales links on my website **a-maverick.com.**

A Maverick Traveller

A funny, interesting compilation of Mary Jane's adventures. Starting from her beginnings in travel it follows her through a life filled with exploration of cultures, mountains, histories and more.

A Maverick New Zealand Way

Finalist in Travel, International Book Awards, 2018. Discover the stunning back country of New Zealand. Come along with Mary Jane on over fifty walks and mountain ascents throughout the islands of New Zealand. Offering an interesting account of New Zealand history and urban development alongside tales of modern-day adventure, it is the perfect read to inspire you to get outdoors in New Zealand.

A Maverick Cuban Way

Trek with Mary Jane to Fidel's revolutionary hideout in the Sierra Maestra. See where the world nearly ended and the Bay of Pigs and have coffee looking at the American Guantánamo Base, all the while doing a salsa to the Buena Vista Social Club.

eason

A Maverick Pilgrim Way

Pilgrim trails are not just for the religious! Follow the winding ancient roads of pilgrims across the continent of Europe and the Mediterranean.

A Maverick USA Way

Mary Jane took Amtrak trains around America and visited Glacier, Yellowstone, Grand Teton, Rocky Mountain and Yosemite National Parks before the snow hit. She loved the Smithsonian museums and after seeing a live dance at the American Indian Museum, she decided to go to Standing Rock. It was a protest over land rights and drinking water, at 30 below zero! She loved Detroit which is going back to being a park, and Galveston and Birmingham, Alabama.

A Maverick Himalayan Way

This was an earlier version of the book that has since become *A Nomad in Nepal,* and of one or two more books in the pipeline!

A Maverick Inuit Way and the Vikings

Mary Jane's adventures in the Arctic take her dog sledding in Greenland, exploring glaciers and icebergs in Iceland, and meeting some interesting locals. She found herself stuck on a ship in the freezing Arctic Ocean amongst icebergs and had her car windows almost blown out by gale force winds! Take a ride through the Arctic and its fascinating history.

Iran: Make Love not War

Finalist in Travel, 14ᵗʰ National Indie Excellence Awards (USA), 2020. Iran is not what you think. It's diverse, culturally rich, and women have more freedoms than you would imagine.

The Scottish Isles: Shetlands, Orkneys and Hebrides (Part 1)

In 2018, Mary Jane decided to tour the islands that lie off the coast of Scotland. She made it around the Orkney and Shetland groups, and to the inner-Hebrides islands of Raasay, Mull, Iona and Staffa as well. She was amazed to discover that Norse influences were as strong as Gaelic ones, indeed stronger on the Orkneys and Shetlands.

Catchy Cyprus: Once was the Island of Love

This is a short book based on Mary Jane's visit to Cyprus, the island that copper's named after. A former British possession in the Mediterranean Sea, Cyprus is divided into Greek-dominated and Turkish-dominated regions with United Nations troops in between.

Lovely Lebanon: A Little Country with a Big History

"I visit the small country of Lebanon, north of Israel, a country whose name means 'the white' in Arabic because of its snow-capped mountains. Lebanon is divided between Christian and Muslim communities and has a history of civil war and invasion. For all that, it is very historic, with lots of character packed into a small space."

Eternal Egypt: My Encounter with an Ancient Land

In this book, Mary Jane explores Egypt, a cradle of civilisation described by the ancient Greek historian Herodotus as the 'gift of the Nile'. Mary Jane put off going to Egypt for years before she finally went. She's glad she did: there's so much more to Egypt than the pyramids!

The Neglected North Island: New Zealand's other half

2021 IPPY Awards Bronze medallist in Australia/New Zealand/Pacific Rim – Best Regional Non-Fiction. Also judged 'Best Antipodean Cultural Travel Book 2021' by *Lux Life* magazine (lux-review.com), *The Neglected North Island* describes New Zealand's other main island: the North Island. The North Island of New Zealand is often overlooked in favour of the mountain scenery of the South Island. Yet it's in the North Island that most of New Zealand's Māori culture is to be found, as well as warm subtropical beauty and Polynesian volcanic landscapes not seen in the chilly south.

The Sensational South Island: New Zealand's Mountain Land

First published in February 2021, *The Sensational South Island* is the companion volume to *The Neglected North Island: New Zealand's other half*. Both books expand on and update *A Maverick New Zealand Way*, which was a finalist in Travel at the International Book Awards, 2018. Mary Jane was born in New Zealand and constantly finds more to explore in her native land!!

For the latest updates on where to get these titles in epub and paperback, see Mary Jane's website and blog on:

a-maverick.com

Made in United States
North Haven, CT
17 March 2022

17241878R00202